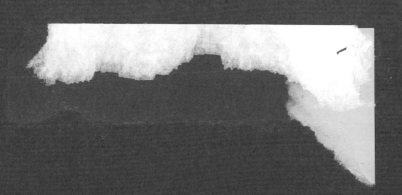

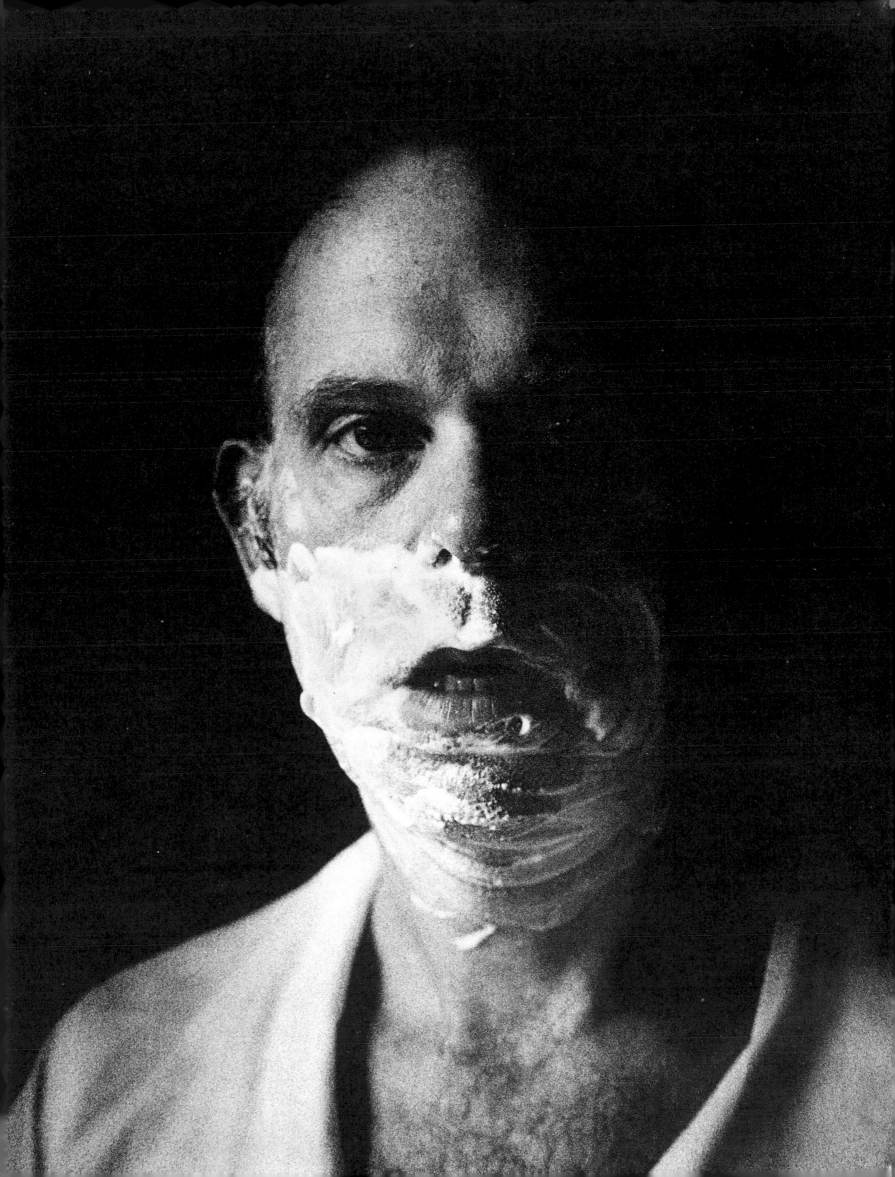

Claes Oldenburg

Drawings and Prints

Introduction and Commentary by Gene Baro

A Paul Bianchini Book

CHELSEA HOUSE PUBLISHERS   LONDON / NEW YORK

Copyright © 1969 by Chelsea House Publishers (London) Limited
All rights reserved under International and Pan-American Copyright Conventions
First published in Great Britain by Chelsea House Publishers (London) Limited
Library of Congress Catalog Card Number 68-8894
Manufactured in Switzerland by Imprimeries Réunies s.a. Lausanne

Contents

Acknowledgments

We gratefully acknowledge the cooperation of the collectors and the museums who provided information, lent their works to be photographed, and granted permission for drawings to be reproduced in this book. Our gratitude is also extended to the following individuals whose information and advice have made this book possible:

Mr. David Anderson, Martha Jackson Gallery, New York
Mrs. Richard Bellamy, New York
Mr. Leo Castelli, New York
Miss Louise Ferrari, Houston.
Miss Marilyn Herzka , New York
Mr. Carroll Janis, Sidney Janis Gallery, New York
Mr. Conrad Janis, Sidney Janis Gallery, New York
Mr. Ivan Karp, New York
Miss Alicia Legg, Museum of Modern Art, New York
Mr. John Powers, Aspen, Colorado
Miss Emily S. Rauh, City Art Museum, St. Louis, Missouri
Mr. Robert Scull, New York
Mr. John Weber, Dwan Gallery, New York
Miss Felice Wender, Dayton's Gallery 12, Minneapolis, Minnesota

Introduction by Gene Baro

With Claes Oldenburg the act of drawing seems wholly natural, a reflex to his inner life and to the world about him. Of course, he draws also quite deliberatively, in preparation for his work in sculpture; but his preoccupation with drawing—or, rather, the ways in which drawing serves his preoccupations—goes well beyond this practical necessity.

Oldenburg fills the interstices of his day with drawing. He draws in the pauses of conversation, and even during talk, when the talk stimulates him. Sitting opposite him, one watches the pen take off across the pages of the small notebooks he always carries. Words and phrases are set down along with images. Sometimes these combinations are intrinsic, sometimes they are the mere associations of the moment. Often, the placement or the treatment is whimsical. These notations may be fragmentary or full. Spontaneity is their pattern. A nervous impulse generates a response that is resolved when the artist turns the page.

This is one sort of drawing activity. Another is the impression Oldenburg brings back to the studio and renders. Such drawings were particularly common around 1958, when Oldenburg spent a good deal of time exploring New York City by bicycle and on foot. He had the habit then of recording in the studio scenes and incidents he had observed in the streets. But sometimes, too, in those days, he carried his notebook along and sketched from life. A few lines of text might accompany these exercises.

Drawings of record have a special character and importance in Oldenburg's *œuvre*. They are the essential visual means by which he confronts and masters the physical world. They are directly and immediately emotional—a response to stimulation within the context of a definite place and a particular mood. They are formal—centered upon the visual structure of things seen in isolation. And they are intellectual—they suggest and sometimes comment upon implications and relationships both visual and verbal.

It is as if Oldenburg were always being surprised into the perception of things. There is the sense in his drawings that the world is being hurried past; the artist grasps his experience as it pulls away from him. This sense of momentary arrest is the basis of the metamorphic power of his sculptures. Even as in the notebook drawings, feeling, formality, and intellectual concerns are fused. A visual image is created that contains and disciplines the fleeting impressions, the fugitive associations and appearances, the free speculations, and invests them structurally in the thing itself. These works seem to hold in suspension everything that has been felt or thought about them.

The notebook drawings and other of Oldenburg's spontaneous graphic exercises are close to his finished drawings and to his sculptures. All share a primary fidelity to physical reality—

to the object; but, also, all project the object as an entity experienced. In short, Oldenburg's works summarize a vision of things as they are and as they seem. Taken individually, they are of a kind. His reaction, his seeing of the thing, is made part of the thing itself.

Fancy, too, is allowed for only as a formal value. With Oldenburg fancy is never used to decorate the form, but is made form itself—is subject to the same fusion as the other elements that go to make up a work. Synthesis is the operable concept.

It is important to remember that Oldenburg's fantasy is centered upon things and upon the states of things. He does not look to dreams or to states of mind for his meanings, but to the visible world. His fantasy is non-symbolic, non-Surrealist. The free play of his imagination is in search of protean forms that are both typical and thematic.

As a child, Oldenburg drew an imaginary country in detail. He included "maps, means of transportation, views of cities, newspapers and magazines, posters for films." Later, an imaginary locale became superfluous. The things of this world in their complexity and shifting aspects provided the central issues to his understanding: what does it look like? what might it be? what is it?

Claes Oldenburg was born January 28, 1929 in Stockholm. His father was a Swedish diplomat, and family life was subject to the vagaries of his assignments. When Claes was three, the Oldenburgs moved to New York City; a year later they were in Oslo for a three-year stay; thereafter, they were in the States again. Their mobility, their being slightly apart from the normal stream of life in the places they lived must have contributed to young Oldenburg's being cast into the role of observer. He must have felt himself between languages and between countries. Is it strange that he should have become concerned with meanings or have developed a sense of the sympathetic interaction of images and of the general unity of forms, given his superb intelligence? With devastating child's logic, belonging to no country, he invented that one of his own.

For a long time, Oldenburg was torn between verbal and visual expression. His earliest ambition was to be a writer. Only gradually did his penchant for drawing begin to lead him firmly toward the vocation of art. In his last two years as a Yale undergraduate (1949-1950), he studied in the School of Fine Arts: Art History, Figure Drawing, Composition. His degree read, "English and Art." Then, there was a strong pull to the verbal. Oldenburg worked two years as an apprentice reporter with the City News Bureau in

Chicago. In 1952, he resumed formal art studies at the Art Institute of Chicago. The following year he interrupted these for a visit to the West Coast. In the autumn of 1953, he lived in San Francisco and Oakland. A few months earlier he had done his first oil paintings at the Oxbow Summer School of Painting in Saugatuck, Michigan. He returned to the Art Institute in 1954. This was his last formal study of art, but his decision was made.

Oldenburg's serious self-education in art, which began when he left the Art Institute, was focused upon drawing. He had painted in the previous year, both in water color and in oil, but drawing was what came to him naturally. Its techniques for creating space conformed to the way in which he saw things. His vision is volumetric; objects appear in middle distance (or at far distance) with air and light, expressed as energy, playing about the forms. Both linear structure and massed tones lend themselves more easily to this kind of vision than painting structure, which relies upon the interaction of flat planes of color.

Studying on his own allowed Oldenburg to systematize his operations in a way that was profoundly congenial to him. His mind is orderly and categorical. His free-ranging imagination is habitually the subject of his own analysis. His understanding that style is itself the imaginative element in art—the fantasy about reality by which the visual world is controlled—led him to draw in all the established and fanciful ways he could think of. These hundreds of drawings, produced from 1954 to 1958 and now mostly destroyed, he criticized, categorized, combined, and re-combined.

He was interested in charting the correspondence of styles to internal and external states and even to the changes of the seasons. He used, for instance, the following formulation:

Objective	*Naturalistic*	*Autumn*
Schizophrenic	*Metamorphic*	*Winter*
Neurotic	*Expressionistic*	*Summer*
Contemplative	*Abstract*	*Spring*

Oldenburg augmented his drawing activity with study in the museums. And he familiarized himself with contemporary art.

In June 1956, he moved to New York, maintaining himself there with a part-time job at the Cooper Union Museum Library. His main occupation continued to be drawing. He did a great many exercises in technique, working in a very small scale. He used imaginary subjects or small things found in the studio, such as razor blades, pencils, and bottle caps.

Late in 1957, Oldenburg rented a larger apartment. This change of abode brought the period of analytical drawing to an end. With room to spare, he began to paint in oil on a large scale, principally nudes and faces. He was concerned now with the analysis of painting styles and techniques. His drawing activity continued and broadened. There were the street drawings mentioned before, the retrospective drawings done in the studio, and the studies for oil paintings.

Friends often posed for Oldenburg at this time. One of his favorite models was Pat Muschinski (later to become his wife); she bore an "uncanny likeness" to his imaginary drawings of faces. Her physical characteristics affected the direction of the drawing. Oldenburg writes: "Pat's movements are rapid and linear, and my drawings changed as a result from a tonal conception suited to painting sketches to a linear one—to an attempt to realize deep space by a tonal line. I settled on a grease crayon as the best instrument for realizing light-space through line."

In fact, Oldenburg was beginning to move away from oil painting by the spring of 1959. His recent experiences with drawing were establishing and confirming the nature of his particular vision. The form in light and space was his central interest. Distance, the sense of the light and air around objects, and sharpness of small detail (as if picked out by light) are crucial terms in his visual idiom. Color is of little importance to this way of seeing.

Of course, the drawings themselves only prefigure the sculptures, where Oldenburg's visual experience is essentialized rather than transcribed. But this comment perhaps is unfair. The visual experience might rather be thought to take place in the immediacy of the drawings. There, the response of eye and hand seems instantaneous and inseparable. This is especially true of Oldenburg's impressionist drawings of 1959, but a majority of the later drawings, too, carry the aura, if not the mark, of impulsive commitment. Even when the drawings have been edited or elaborated by the artist, the sense of the initial engagement remains. There are relatively few exceptions; among them are the pattern drawings for sculptures and the drawings refinished to meet some special purpose, such as translation into the print medium.

What I have called the impressionist drawings were done by Oldenburg in the summer of 1959 at Lenox, Massachusetts. These were mainly drawings of Pat Muschinski in domestic and studio settings. He also did then a remarkable series of landscapes, in which the energies of the crayon line suggest, in the same stroke, both the masses of objects and the immaterial lightness of atmosphere.

When Oldenburg returned to the city in the autumn, he also turned away from the free description of the Lenox drawings. He was to make the city itself, the life of the street, his theme. The idea had been with him for some time. In 1958, when he had been categorizing drawings in an attempt to judge their dominant characteristics, he had also separated them according to themes. The City (what was to become "The Street") was one of these. The summer away had finished a phase of work for him and had confirmed him in the sense that the street was his "most affecting environment." In addition, he had reached the decision to abandon oil painting and to work in three dimensions. This was a great turning point in every way, a giving in to himself.

Part of the change was marked by a search for "techniques more expressive of the subject." Attitude must somehow be made to serve as a term in a visual paradigm. Oldenburg writes: "I turned my vision down—the paper became a metaphor for the pavement, its walls (gutters and fences). I drew the materials found on the street—including the human. A person on the street is more of the street than he is human."

There were a number of influences in this development that Oldenburg acknowledges: the example of Dubuffet, his reading of Celine's Mort à Crédit, and, more immediately, the drawings of Jim Dine and Red Grooms. But the city itself provided the compelling context. Oldenburg was living on the Lower East Side, and the life of that depressed area, particularly its onward-rushing character, is reflected and essentialized in Oldenburg's work. He writes: "The drawing at this time takes on an 'ugliness' which is a mimicry of the scrawls and patterns of street graffiti. It celebrates irrationality, disconnection, violence and stunted expression—the damaged life forces of the city street."

The style of Oldenburg's "Street" period (autumn 1959-spring 1960) is essentially linear and tonal. The materials used have a certain roughness, both in the drawings (cardboard, wood, turpentine wash) and in the constructions (strips of newspaper dipped in wheat paste and laid on chicken wire). The effect is metamorphic; unresolved images and disintegrating forms suggest their own obliteration. The objects seem to be wearing away; the scrawls look about to fade; and the figures appear both stained and staining. An important element in this work is writing and lettering, the emphasis upon signs and messages (even the use of newspaper or magazine copy as materials of collage). Here, the incompleteness of the communication is part of the larger visual intention—the sense of all that slips or falls away. On the street, we pass and are passed in turn.

The Street was to be a continuing theme for Oldenburg. He returned to it a number of times (as late as 1967) after it had ceased to be his dominant interest. In the summer of 1960, he seemed to be leaving it for all time. That summer he spent in Provincetown, Massachusetts, on Cape Cod. He was tired of the rigors and intensities of New York. Oldenburg writes that the summer away was "intended as an obliteration by non-city nature of my involvement with the city street." He took a job dishwashing in a restaurant. The experience, the techniques involved in restaurant work, the array of objects dealt with, stimulated him and moved his mind in the direction of his next considerable creative effort, The Store.

A journal entry of the period, June 29, 1960, provides valuable insight into Oldenburg's way of engaging and assimilating new materials. The combination of systematic study and free association gives him the greatest flexibility in using his visual experience; at the same time, he is able to emphasize continuity. He writes:

> *The aims of drawing on arrival in a new environment. Forms are carried along, the result of having found one's forms in other environments. Now one must find the meaningful, i.e., typical or thematic forms in the new environment and then bring them together with the brought forms.*

> *First: a period of discovery, both as to technique (surface and tool, treatment, etc. of the typical forms). Second: their poetic merger, metamorphosis, and relationship thru association. The poetic symbol, the "image." Drawing is attained in a new place when the old has been expanded with the new, association is operating well—showing the family relationship of the forms, the unity of things in general, and when the proper technique has been developed to present the expanded and particularized as to place, poetic vision.*

> *This period is very unsatisfying... one is reborn, rather must reintegrate and develop the new relation in a natural way to one's new surroundings, so that they may spear directly thru one.*

Beginning with the Street, Oldenburg's work has developed through a series of inclusive images or spatial forms into which other, smaller images, forms, and processes have fit. The Street, the Store, the Home, even the Airflow is a particular space articulated by the various elements it is made to contain. In the case of the drawings, the larger form is the paper area or surface, given spatial meaning by the several individual forms discovered there and, of course, by their relationships.

In the Provincetown period (summer 1960), the dominating image was the American flag. Oldenburg had been struck by the commercialization of American history and of patriotic feeling in this resort. But, also, the rectangularity of the flag—its definiteness as an area and its variability of shape, texture, and color as commonly seen—had a strong visual appeal. In effect, the flag was a collage, a combination of elements creating a field.

The flag image also related to some of the work done the previous autumn and winter, large drawings with torn paper edges, some double-sided and hung perpendicular to the wall. The literalness of these drawings suggested the arbitrariness of the flag image. In July, Oldenburg writes: "Drawing that is actual, that is concrete, that is what is achieved by the torn line. And not achieved by the drawn line. This is it. Only this in drawing gives me satisfaction." The desire to "draw" in construction was no doubt behind these remarks (often Oldenburg's most telling drawing is within his finished sculpture). In Province-town, between June and August, he made a series of flags out of driftwood and other found materials. Again, the materials were coarse, and the color—echoing the topography, color, and texture of the Cape—ran to browns, blacks, and greys. "The silhouettes of the dunes appear in the irregular stripes of some 'flags.' "

At the same time, the flag image was beginning to move Oldenburg away from the linear and tonal techniques of the Street and from his preoccupation with coarse materials and apparent lack of finish. A number of the drawings of the summer are concerned with color. Also, the flag begins to suggest the possibilities of cloth as a sculptural material.

Autumn 1960 was a period of gestation and transition for Oldenburg. Back in New York, he did a series of angular drawings of street figures and of street figures combined with flags; color was added to some of these. His notebook drawings gradually became centered upon store goods, particularly clothing. Later in the autumn he began doing water colors of store windows, an activity that continued into 1961. He had been asked to design costumes for the Aileen Pasloff Dance Company; this commission provided another stimulus to color and to the serious consideration of the potentialities of fabric.

The previous March Oldenburg had become involved in the performance of a Happening, "Snapshots from the City" at the Judson Gallery. He was to have a continuing interest in this kind of theatrical activity. "Blackouts" was performed in the Reuben Gallery in December: Oldenburg's notebooks of the late autumn are rich in costume and theatre sketches.

The Store projects and the theatre works are closely related. They are both involved in a stylistic shift from the linear to the coloristic. The Store drawings are developed from "areas of atmospheric wash set in space with a summary indication of line (usually a cast shadow or the space-energizing dots)... the paper becomes the Store window." In fact, the

Store window may be regarded as an analogue of the proscenium arch, and the Store itself as a surrogate stage. The coloring of the Store drawings is a form of stage lighting: "atmospheric wash... space-energizing dots" suggest the kind of illusion made with footlights, spots, and gelatins. And the Store relief and objects are a wire armature "dressed" in stiffened fabric and painted; in one sense décor, in another the elements of the visual drama.

Oldenburg's Store was in three versions. The first, made up mostly of reliefs, was part of an exhibition, "Environments, Situations, Spaces," at the Martha Jackson Gallery (May-June 1961). The second and more important, with many new pieces in three dimensions, was arranged by the artist himself, in an actual store he had rented as a studio. It is of interest that these premises doubled as a theatre*. The third version indicated a changed concept and must be discussed separately.

In the spring of 1962, the dealer Richard Bellamy offered Oldenburg the use of the Green Gallery on Fifty-Seventh Street for the summer, for the purpose of building a one-man show there. The midtown environment was new to Oldenburg. He was stimulated to make a number of drawings visualizing Fifty-Seventh Street and future exhibit. In the latter, "the space of the drawing... becomes the space of a gallery, a move toward anonymity of space, and a concentration on the objects themselves... Drawing in space required an emphasis on volume. This was stimulated by stuffed pieces made as props and costumes for the Ray Gun Theatre performances—which led to the 'soft' sculptures."

Oldenburg's serious exploration of volume begins with the preparations for the Green Gallery show. The primary impetus comes from his sense of the space to be filled—not from the perception of physical dimension or area, but from an intuition of the nature of the spatial experience. The objects seem to suggest themselves; they are in the idiom of the Store, but have a simplicity that emphasizes their largeness of scale as structural ideas and the ambiguity of their surroundings. The visualization drawings for the exhibition have great freedom, but also convey specificity. The object is very much to the fore, a quality that translates into the canvas 'soft' objects of the exhibition.

In 1962-1963, Oldenburg elaborated the volumetric style. Rounded or pneumatic subjects were preferred. In the drawings, shapes bulged "by a scalloping, convex line about the object." But the soft sculptures (now in vinyl) that derived from these imaginative descriptions required design precision for their proper realization. Their relaxed look was a matter

* Performances of Oldenburg's Ray Gun Theatre took place in The Store, 107 East Second Street.

of meeting structural requirements exactly. The problem of making patterns and templates led Oldenburg to develop a style allied to mechanical drawing, "involving the use of perspective, but thoroughly flat."

In August 1963, he gave up The Store and moved to Venice, California. It was here that his mechanical style matured. The imagined space of the drawings becomes a room, and the social setting becomes The Home. The work of this period culminates in the "Bedroom Ensemble," the famous quasi-realist construction shown as part of the "4 Environments" exhibition, at the Sidney Janis Gallery, January 1964.

The next major stylistic shift occured when Oldenburg reestablished himself in New York after spending several months in Europe. This was in March 1965. He had acquired a huge studio, 204 feet in length, and had opened up the rooms so that he could see from one end to the other. The size of this place, plus his experience of air travel over the previous months, fixed his attention upon the subject of scale. He began the "monument" drawings, in which the operable space is a landscape. The view is at a distance and is usually aerial. "Colossal" as applied to these monuments implies that the landscape is intended as actual.

Oldenburg writes:

> *A large part of the pleasure of drawing is the awareness of shifting scale. Drawing is miniaturistic, but while drawing one imagines differences of scale. One effect of the monument drawings is an imaginary expansion of the drawing scale. The function of these drawings is to depict, like an impressionist photograph, though there are elements of unnaturalistic calligraphy recalling the line drawings of 1959.*
>
> *The 'monuments'—a conceptual direction—move from simple placement of favorite objects onto the landscape to more studied relations of object and site, for example, the ironing board echoes the shape of Manhattan island. Some of the juxtapositions are means to social comment, often supported by written material accompanying the drawings. Some "drawings" consist of text alone, a sort of prose-poetry describing a visual effect.*

This series of drawings and the projects related to it occupied Oldenburg intermittently during 1966 and 1967. His principal monument activity centered upon New York, Chicago, Toronto, Stockholm, and London. The invention almost always involved a real environment; occasionally, there would be a monument whose site was imagined, but always the site would be some recognizable feature of the urban landscape, usually a park. Though the monuments are in a sense literary in conception and provoke discussion and explanation, their abiding strength is visual. They remain in the mind as images. This ability to discipline his ideas to the eye is the typical feature of Oldenburg's genius.

During 1965-1967, Oldenburg engaged upon a number of important projects apart from the monument series. Of course, he is always preparing for particular exhibitions, and a coherent body of work will group around each exhibition's theme. Moreover, there are always drawings being made in preparation for or in imaginative anticipation of sculptures. These various kinds of work may take place more or less simultaneously. Sometimes different projects will be in different styles. For instance, while the monument style (and concern) might be thought to dominate a period, Oldenburg was also working in quite another way within the same span. In 1966, he worked on the Airflow and the following year produced the "Drainpipes," "Giant Fag Ends," "Giant Fan," and "Giant Soft Drum Set." In 1967 also, there was a shift in the drawings toward the human figure. Oldenburg did a series of erotic pencil drawings that treated the figure as an object. These echoed certain earlier erotic drawings of his.

For Oldenburg, style has come to be another tool in the mastery of form, a servant of perceptual insight, a vehicle of feeling. He writes:

> *Style means to me a clear and consistent method as to material and technique, for rendering a definite state of mind and correlative subject. A practical and functional solution which may or may not draw on previous styles (mine or others'). A style period is preceded by analysis. Once begun, it assembles all relevant elements in a consistency, as, for example, the paper becomes the street (a floor—downward glance), or wall (a window—sidelong glance), or room (deep glance), or unbounded atmosphere (deeper glance).*

> *The periods of the Street, Store, and Home are systematic explorations of, successively: Line-Plane, Color, Volume—an analysis of elements of drawing, using correlative subjects in my immediate surroundings.*

The role that draughtsmanship has played in the shaping of Oldenburg's artistic intelligence can scarcely be exaggerated. Drawing in all its forms has been of the first importance to the sculpture of this master. Drawing has helped Oldenburg to go beyond the traditional sculptural concept to the idea of the formal and spiritual complexity of objects and of their intercommunication. But if the drawings seem to serve a purpose, they have also a telling force and integrity on their own. They are the tissue and substance of a vision, brought alive with a technical control, wit, and freedom second to none.

Note: all quotations are from unpublished writings of Claes Oldenburg.

Selected Drawings and Prints

1 STREET EVENT—WOMAN BEATING CHILD 1958
Pen and watercolor, 7½×5 in.
The artist, New York

In 1958 Oldenburg did much walking in the streets of New York and,
on returning to the studio, set down incidents he had witnessed.

2 CIRCUS GIRL ON BIG BALL 1958
Crayon, 6¾× 5 in.
The artist, New York

Sketch done after attending the circus. The interesting element
here is the fusion of ball and body. The linking of objects is
a persistent device. (See Nº 42, *Material and Scissors*, 1963.)

6   PAT IN BLACK UNDERWEAR, SEATED   1959
Crayon, 14×10¾ in.
Gene Baro, London, England

One of many studies for paintings made in 1959. The emphasis was
on tonality. The model was posed against windows covered with
paper, which diffused the light. The model was asked to wear black
clothes. In these drawings, an important element is the white area
of thigh delimited by the contours of garter belt and stocking.

8 PAT LYING WITH LEGS APART IN SLIP 1959
Crayon, 10×13¾ in.
The artist, New York

An early drawing of Oldenburg's wife in which he tried
to reduce a gestural posture to a planar composition.

9 PAT, NUDE, IN CHAIR, WITH BLACK BAND AROUND WAIST 1959
Crayon, 8¾ × 11⅞ *in.*
Mrs. Claes Oldenburg, New York

Oldenburg did a number of drawings using the black band, introducing
a linear element in "real" space, "like the stroke of a lithographic
crayon in air." In this drawing, more than in some of the others of the
period, there is an attempt at characterization. The fixed stare is
used as a counterbalance to the curves of the chair and the body.

10   PAT, BENT FORWARD, SHAKING HER HAIR DOWN   1959
     Crayon, 14×16⅝ *in.*
     The artist, New York

This is one of the many drawings of Oldenburg's wife
done in early 1959 as preparatory studies for paintings.

12 PAT STANDING, FROM SIDE—"MONKEY WOMAN" 1959
Crayon, 35 × 23½ in.
The artist, New York

An early example of Oldenburg's linear style. He was
experimenting with the reduction of the face to the simplest
components that could still give a sense of life.

13 PAT, NUDE, SEATED, FROM BEHIND 1959
      Crayon, 13⅝ × 10 in.
      The artist, New York

A chief interest for Oldenburg in this drawing was
to express volume in a single plane without sacrificing
the overall flow of the free line to modeling.

14 PAT, NUDE, SLEEPING WITH CAT 1959
Crayon, 10×13¾ *in.*
The artist, New York

Animal studies from life are rare in Oldenburg's work; when they occur
they are usually of cats. He prefers cats because they are "fast-moving
and linear, full of surprises, a description which may also be applied to my
wife." The drawing, tense in itself, treats these energized forms at rest.

15　PAT SEATED, WITH HAIR OVER HER FACE　1959
Crayon, 11¾ × 17½ *in.*
The artist, New York

After making studies in the tonal style, Oldenburg turned to
representing space by line. This approach led away from painting and
began for him a period of setting space in vibration by linear accents.
In these drawings, light is conceived as energy rather than as illusion.

16 PAT, WITH PIGTAIL, FROM BEHIND, IN LENOX STUDIO 1959
Crayon, 14×16½ *in.*
The artist, New York

This drawing was made in a country shed that served as
Oldenburg's studio. It marks the beginning of a shift from figural
to landscape interest. The figure is reduced, along with the other
details of costume and surroundings, to generalized plant forms.

19 HOUSE BETWEEN TREES, CASTING A SHADOW, LENOX 1959
Crayon, 12 × 17½ in.
Provenance : 5 ; Dayton's Gallery 12, Minneapolis, Minnesota
Paul Bianchini, New York

Oldenburg summered in Lenox, Massachusetts in 1959. He made
this drawing late in the season when his attention had shifted from
figure studies to landscape. In landscape he found the
possibility of achieving a grander, more monumental space.

In the present drawing the emphasis is upon light as the maker of space;
shadow is part of the literal structure. The drawing's metamorphic
effects were accidental and surprising. In his search for openness,
Oldenburg reduced what he saw to a calligraphy of bare indications.

26 STREET POEM—MOON POP 1959
   Ink, 18 × 16¼ in.
   The artist, New York

A visual poem, in the style of children's street poems. The
background was rollered in imitation of both the look and the
preparation of asphalt and of the action of passing automobile tires.

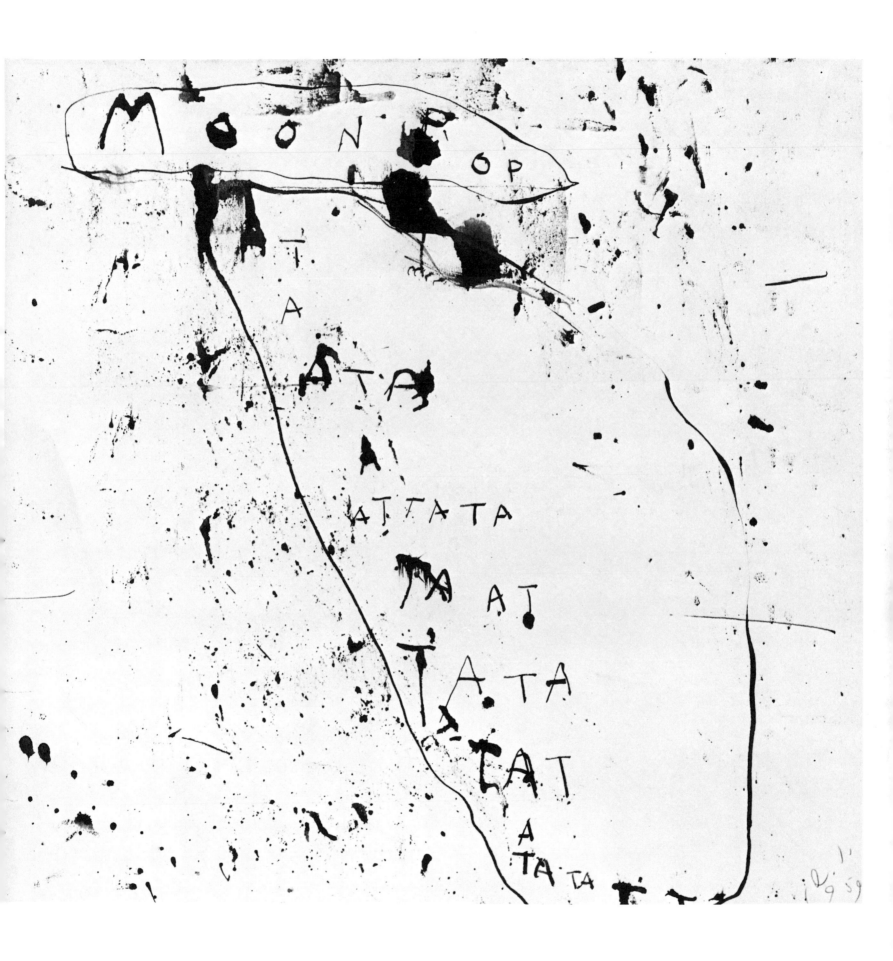

30 DUBUFFET-CELINE-FRENCHMEN 1959
Ink, 16¼ × 11¾ in.
Provenance : 4
Collection of Mr. and Mrs. Robert C. Scull, New York

An irregular "ripped" drawing, acknowledging the influence
of the street drawings of Dubuffet and Céline's novel *Mort
à Crédit (Death on the Installment Plan)*. These works enabled
Oldenburg to shape his response to the desperate civilization
of the streets, a preoccupation of his at this time.

31   RAY GUN POSTER—AIRPLANE FACE   1960
Monoprint, 17¾ × 11⅞ in.
The artist, New York

A poster made on newsprint, intended to be fixed to walls in the
neighborhood of the Ray Gun show. Oldenburg made the poster
to announce the show; an important interest for him was to see
how it weathered and survived accidental effects of its exposure.

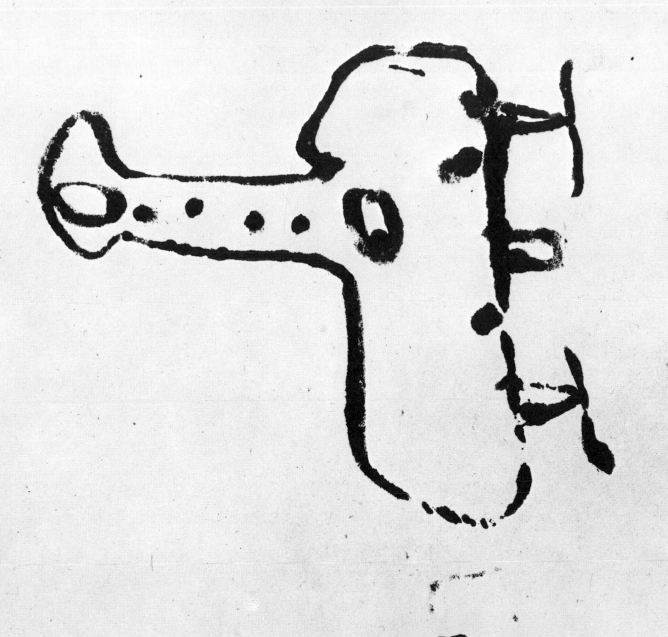

RAY GUN

This is one of a series of metamorphic figures based upon
analysis of teen-age girls walking to school and loitering on the
Lower East Side. It reflects elements of fashion of that time,
for example, enormous eccentric shoes, long full hair, and severe
eye make-up. It also reflects the emphasis of the period on legs, which
reduced interest in the torso—a tendency toward a phallic image.

51   ORIGINAL FOR ANNOUNCEMENT, REUBEN GALLERY ONE-MAN SHOW   1960
Ink on newspaper, 13½ × 10¼ *in.*
The artist, New York

This poster can be read either way as a vertical, but not as a
horizontal; the intention was to work against the conventional
type line. Three street figures are shown; they are deployed
as if walking on opposite sides of a street.

52   YA BLA AND MAN IN CAR   1960
     Monoprint, 24×18 in.
     The artist, New York

     One of a number of drawings in the Reuben Gallery show which
     attempted to bring in the mumblings and expletives of the street.
     Representing them in the cartoon style of balloons made them
     as concrete as the Street objects themselves. This is "heard" language
     as compared with the visible language of the street signs.

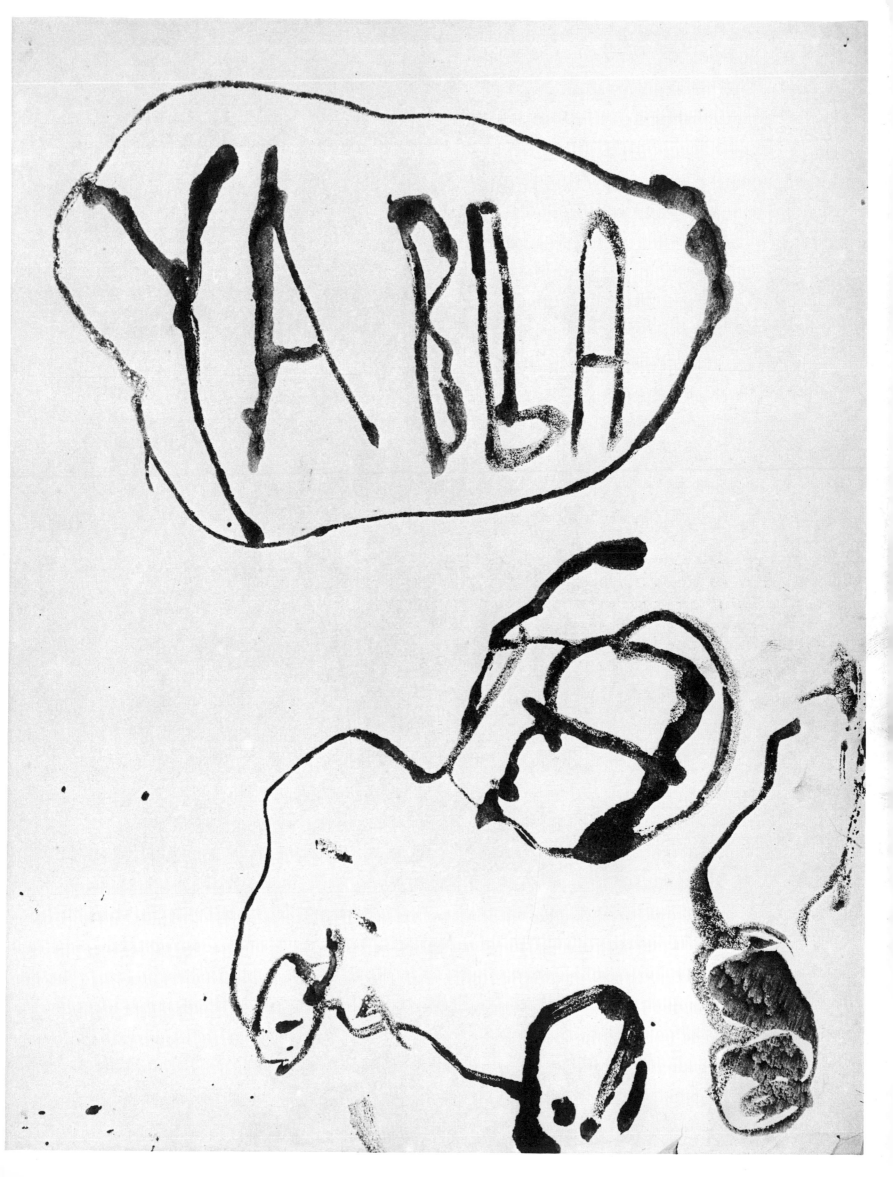

53 TENEMENT, EMPIRE SIGN, AND AIRPLANE 1960
Monoprint, 24×18 in.
The artist, New York

A drawing on the Street theme shown at the Reuben Gallery in 1960.
The stripes on the tenement are fire escapes, and the images which
appear to be bombs are windows. The style of drawing associated with
the Street was the result of a fascination with children's drawing and
street graffiti of all kinds, which Oldenburg did not literally copy
but identified with. The unclosed, loose quality of street graffiti
attracted him and suggested the projection of drawings into sky space.

54 VAN 1960
Cardboard, oil wash, and wood, 12¼ × 13 in.
Mrs. Claes Oldenburg, New York

Drawing as object. Originally on the wall of the Judson Ray
Gun Street, an environmental exhibition of January, 1960.

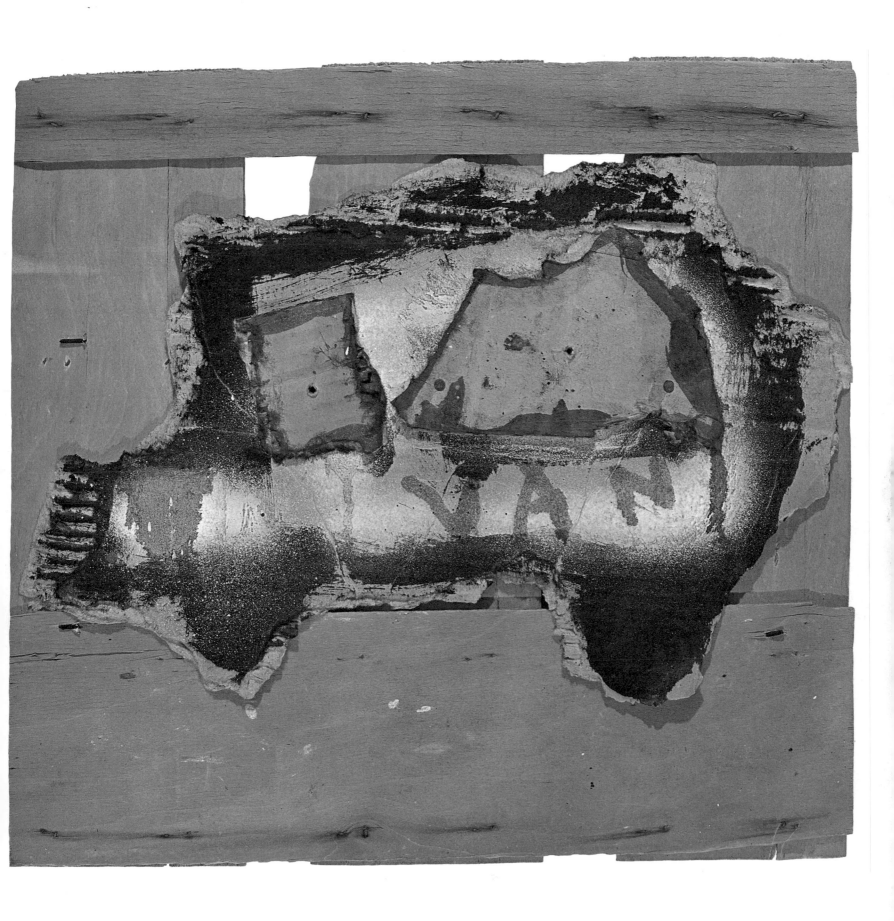

55   CAR ON A FRAGMENT OF STREET   1960
Cardboard, oil wash, and spray enamel, 13½ × 31½ *in.*
The artist, New York

Originally made for the Judson Ray Gun show held in January, 1960,
where it was mounted on the wall of the Ray Gun Street; reshaped and
remounted for the Reuben Gallery one-man show in May, 1960.
At this time Oldenburg made a point of using materials found on the
street, treated in the neutral colors of the street. He used the
"techniques" of the street: in making his drawings he imitated random,
casual, but ever-present street phenomena, "such as piss
running across a sidewalk, flowing gutter water, falling dirt."

56 STREET FRAGMENT WITH CAR AND GIRL WALKING 1960
Cardboard, paper, and turpentine wash, with movable "leg", 31×22 in.
The artist, New York

This drawing is unusual in that it has a moving part,
the leg of the walker. It is typical of the period in that the
image is ripped out of paper and hung in space.

58 EMPIRE SIGN—WITH M AND I DELETED 1960
Cardboard and oil wash, 54½× 23¾ in.
The artist, New York

This sign is one of several large drawings based upon movie
marquees and other signs projecting over streets. The originals of
such signs suggested drawings suspended in space, which
particularly interested Oldenburg at the time. (See Nº 56, *Street
Fragment with Car and Girl Walking*, 1960). The top of the marquee
contains a plus and a minus sign. The shape seems both phallic
and a forerunner of the Mickey Mouse variations.

59 STREET SIGN 1960
Cardboard and oil wash, both sides, 104×41½ in.
The artist, New York

This two-sided drawing, meant to be
hung at right angles to the wall, is again
based upon a conglomeration of words
read on street signs, for example, *now,*
Orpheum, Empire, Romeo, and the
name of a Polish wrestler, *Zybysko.*

68

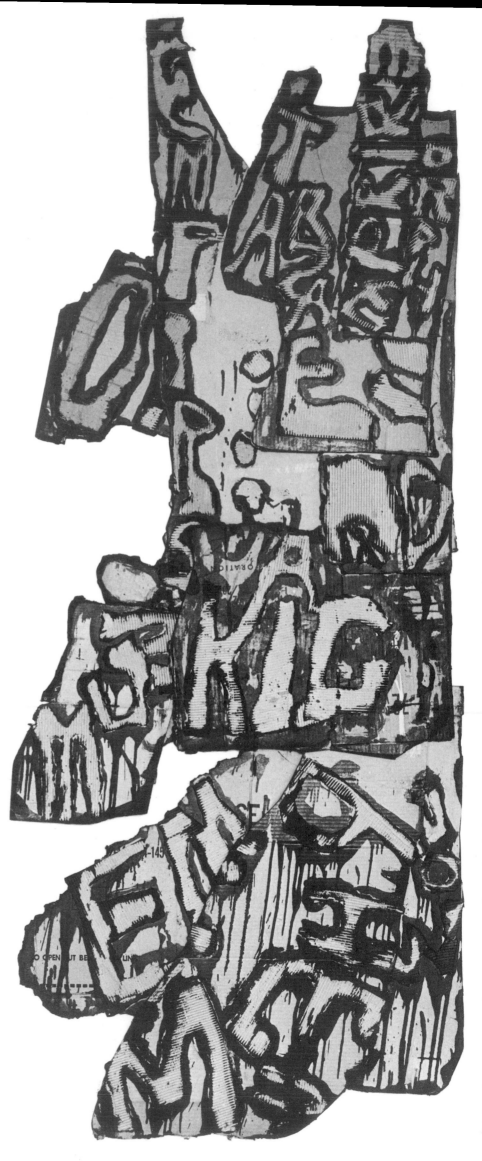

62 POSTER—"NEW MEDIA, NEW FORMS I," MARTHA JACKSON GALLERY 1960
Photoengraving (original lost), 22 ⁵/₈ × 17 ³/₄ in.
The artist, New York

Oldenburg was commissioned by the Martha Jackson Gallery to make
a poster containing the names of all the artists of this large show of
newcomers. The solution presents an Indian "who may or may not be
Martha Jackson." The names are the feathers in her headdress but
the image is also a shoe on a foot and a penis—a mysterious image.

64 FLAG TO FOLD IN THE POCKET 1960
Ink, 29½×47 in. (unfolded)
The artist, New York

One of a number of studies of flags made by Oldenburg during the
summer of 1960. He was living then in Provincetown, Massachusetts,
and working in a restaurant. The present drawing was made upon
butcher paper used for wrapping meat in the restaurant kitchen. The
paper was already wrinkled with use; Oldenburg wrinkled it further
and made the drawing in the spirit of a primitive map. He then
folded it. The idea was that the drawing be carried in the pocket to
be taken out and unfolded at the end of one's walk or journey.

69   NUDE FIGURE WITH AMERICAN FLAG—A B C HOORAY   1960
Ink and watercolor, 11 × 8½ in.
Mrs. Claes Oldenburg, New York

This is among the several drawings done in late 1960 which serve
as a transition between the quasi-figurative work of the Street and the
object images of the Store. Also, it shows the transition from line
to color as an interest. The Street drawings are mainly watercolors.
This drawing is the declaration of Oldenburg's new interest.

70 SKETCH FOR A SCENE IN A PERFORMANCE 1960
Crayon and pencil, 11 × 8½ in.
The artist, New York

A visualization of an event in a Happening that Oldenburg
was preparing, which involved the placing of the figure in a
sacrificial posture on a rock. The denseness of the atmosphere
in the drawing indicates the theatrical effect intended, and
the vagueness of the figure the possibility of movement.

sketch for a play

72 STUDY USING AN AMERICAN FLAG 1960
Chalk and crayon, 13½×10 in.
The artist, New York

From the early Store period. An attempt to
visualize the appearance of the Store reliefs.

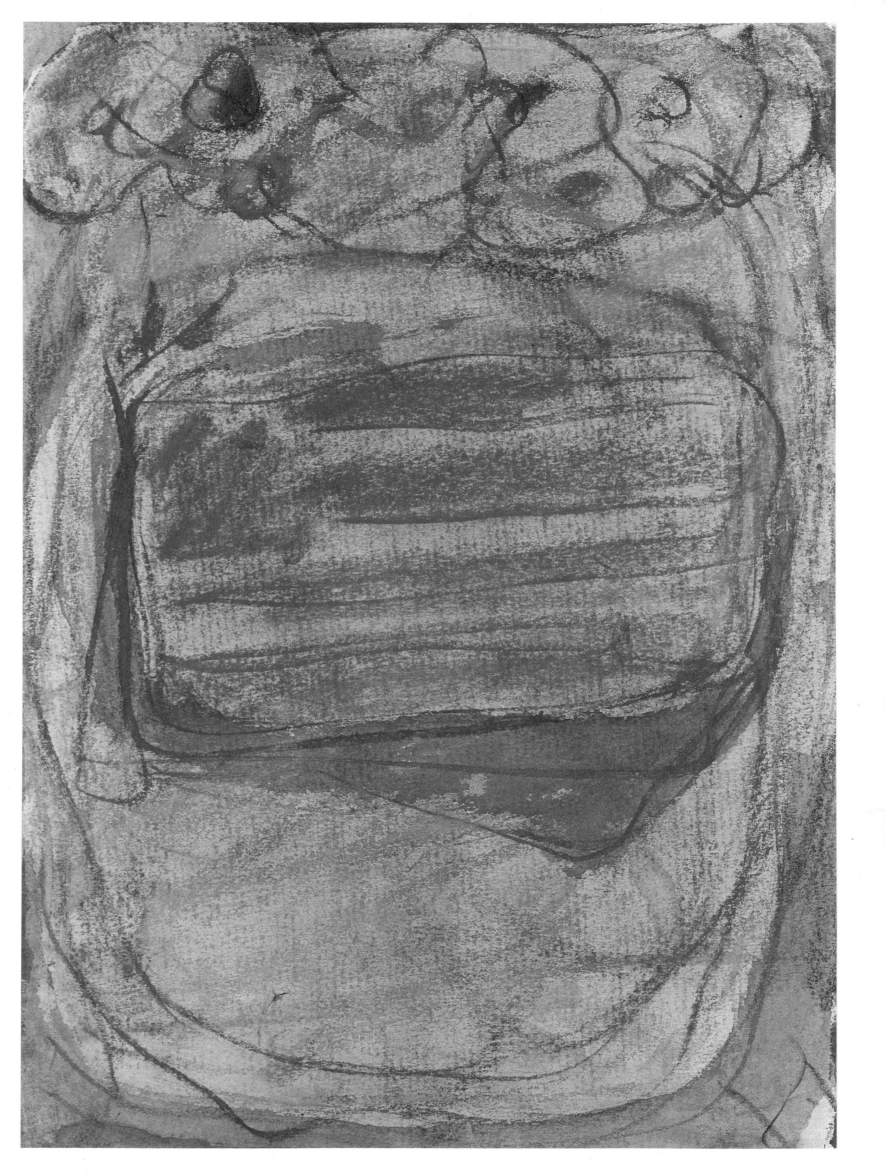

73 OBJECTS FROM THE WINDOW OF A LINGERIE SHOP—GIRDLE,
STOCKINGS, BRA 1960
Ink, 8¾ × 6¼ in.
The artist, New York

A drawing early in the phase of drawing objects, Store objects, in
the window situation. Here, the linear and metamorphic style of the
Street has not yet been changed into a more literal representation.

74 STREET CHICK FROM THE SIDE, AS IF IN WINDOW, WITH
FORTY-NINE CENTS SIGN 1960
Chalk and pencil, 11 × 8½ in.
The artist, New York

One of the drawings made in the early period of the Store. It is
conceived as a window full of light and objects as seen from the street.
The figure in this phase is reduced to doll-like or mannequin form.

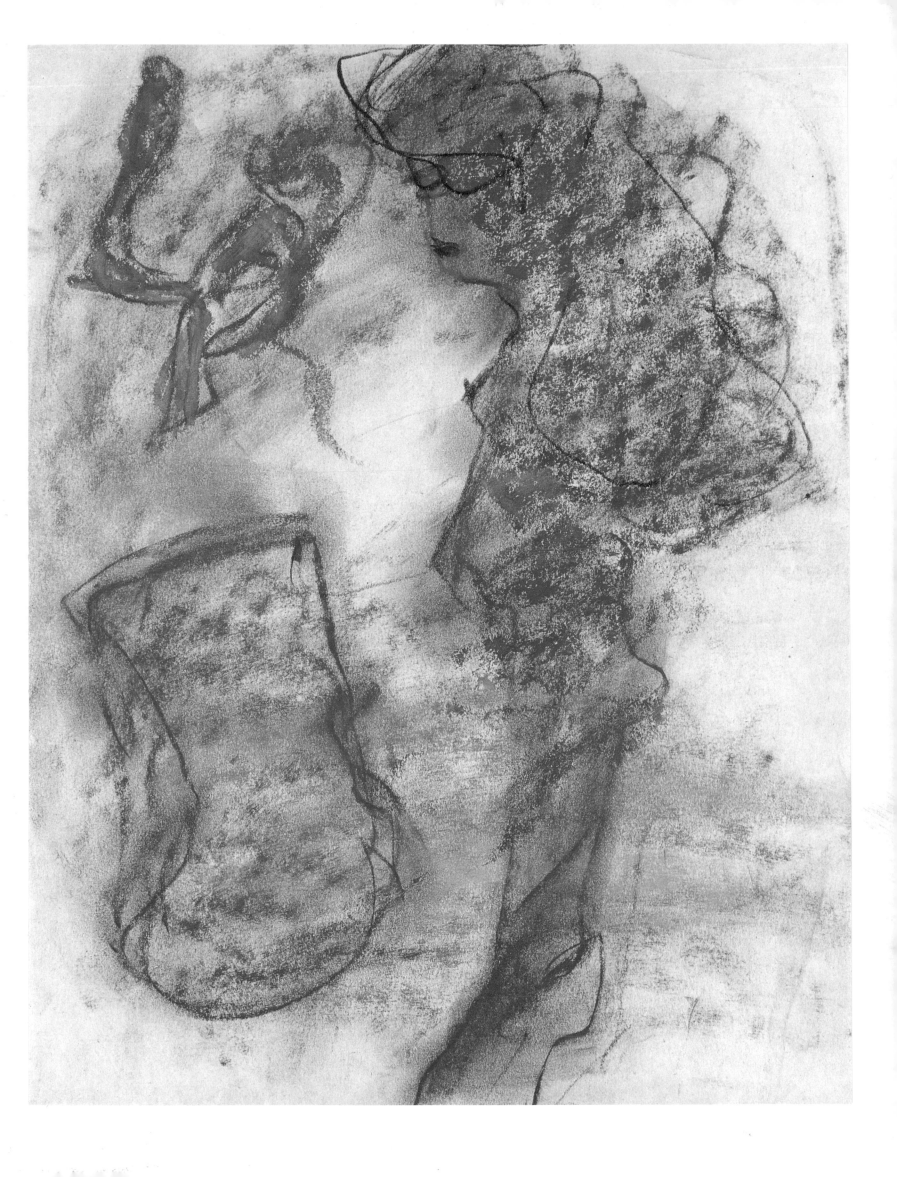

75 POSTER FOR A PROJECTED PERFORMANCE—INJUN 1960
Monoprint and watercolor, 16¾ × 13⅞ in.
The artist, New York

A poster made to announce a performance whose events were inspired
by incidents from American history, a preoccupation of Oldenburg's
in the period just before the Store. (Compare with Nº 62, Martha
Jackson poster, 1960.)

76 POSTER FOR "BLACKOUTS"—BUTTER AND JAM 1960
Monoprint, 16¾ × 13⅛ in.
The artist, New York

A poster announcing one of the sections of Oldenburg's
second Happening. It was used in the same way as a sign
announcing an act in a vaudeville theatre or music hall.

BUTTER AND JAM

2 LEGS 1961

Etching, 11⅛ × 15 in.

Edition : 12
Printed at Pratt Center for Contemporary Printmaking, New York
Publisher : The artist
Signed C.O. 1961 in pencil at the bottom center and numbered from 1 to 12 at the bottom center

Oldenburg frequently isolates the drawn object or image from its
normal surroundings and containing space. In the neutral space of his
presentation, both the formal and evocative elements of the subject are
emphasized. But also, literalness is played down by the very absence of
context, the reverse of the Pop art device that presents the object or
images as super-real. In this etching, Oldenburg has translated the
essentials of a drawing style into the requirements of the press medium.

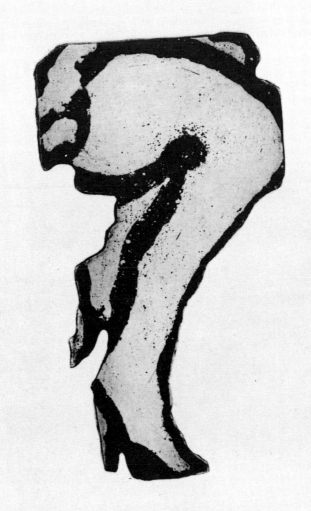

2nd ed. 8/12 . Legs   C.D. 1961

3 ORPHEUM SIGN 1961

Etching, 10 × 7⅝ in.
Edition: 100
Printed at Georges Leblanc, Paris, in brown-black and scratched on surface
Note: Six artist proofs printed at Pratt Center, 1961, in blue-black on paper 11⅛ × 15 in., signed A.P. and numbered from 1 to 6
Publisher: Galeria Schwarz, Milan, Italy
Signed Claes O. in pencil at the bottom center and numbered from 1 to 100

This etching relates both to Oldenburg's Street drawings and to his drawings involving torn papers. The plate is burned away to leave the image, quite as if it had been ripped out of the metal. The "sign" makes a play of its formal elements and suggests a continuing impression of street signs, isolated against blank façades or seen against the sky.

Orpheum sign   A.P. I ⁹⁄₆ Clee.O.

78 SKETCH FOR A DANCE COSTUME—BLUE DISCS, BIG RED HAT 1961
Pencil and watercolor, 10 × 7 ½ in.
The artist, New York

At the beginning of 1961, Oldenburg was asked to do costumes for the Aileen Passloff Dance Company. He tried to render the costume conceptions not merely as working sketches but as drawings in themselves.

88 NOTEBOOK SKETCH—FRAGMENT OF A BATHROOM WALL, WITH BATHTUB 1961
Crayon on steno-paper, mounted on sheet, 11 × 8½ in.
The artist, New York

In 1961, out of experiences with Lower East Side bathrooms,
Oldenburg had planned a piece in the fragment style of that period.
The work was intended to include the bathtub and a section of wall,
in relief rendering. This piece was not executed, but Oldenburg
made a complete bathtub as a soft sculpture in the Home period, 1966.

89 NOTEBOOK SKETCH—STOCKINGS DISPLAY 1961
Pencil and watercolor, 11 × 8½ in.
The artist, New York

One of the window drawings on a notebook page. The interest
is in the shifting planes of a flat stocking arranged for display.

90   NOTEBOOK SKETCH—GYM SHOES   1961
Ink, 4¾×3 in.
The artist, New York

A drawing from a window display on 14th Street.

91 THINGS IN A WINDOW—OVOIDS AND A CUBE 1961
   Crayon, 12⅛ × 10½ in.
   The artist, New York

A sketch for a Store announcement, presented as if the
objects were seen in a window. The address is that of The Store.

99 STUDIES FOR STORE OBJECTS—PIE, 7-UP, FLAG, ORANGES, FIFTEEN CENTS 1961
Collage, crayon, and watercolor, 15×20 in.
Mr. and Mrs. Burton G. Tremaine, New York

Assemblages such as this one relate to Oldenburg's plaster
and enamel wall reliefs, which mimic torn paper edges. They
can be regarded as miniature studies for putting together
the diverse forms of the major wall pieces such as the Store
clusters. The originals of the scraps are torn from newspapers.

108 CAP 1961
Monoprint and watercolor, 24×18 in.
The artist, New York

A Store object, later realized as a sculpture. The "cap" stands for Claes
And Pat, expressing the collaboration of husband and wife,
particularly marked in the Store period. When the interest of the
drawings settled upon objects, it became an idiosyncrasy to include the
calligraphic description of an object in words within the drawing.

109   RAY GUN POSTER   1961
Sprayed oil wash on torn paper, 24×18 in.
The artist, New York

Poster made to announce the Ray Gun show at the Judson Gallery.
The technique involves the concept of the reversal of figure
and field and the association of light and dark, earth and sky.

III STORE POSTER 1961
Dripped and pressed enamel, 12 × 17½ *in.*
The artist, New York

One of the first attempts at an announcement for the Store. A
calligraphic use of the materials of which the Store objects were made.

113 STUDY FOR ANNOUNCEMENT OF DANCE CONCERT BY AILEEN PASSLOFF DANCE
COMPANY—DANCING FIGURE 1962
Dripped enamel, 17½×12 in.
The artist, New York

Representation of a dancing figure, where the dripped enamel
is freely used as in a dance movement. Aileen Passloff's name is
written across the poster; the poster was rejected for illegibility.
There is a tension between the poster as drawing and the poster as
information. Oldenburg usually settles for the poster as drawing.

117   STORE OBJECTS—WATCH IN CASE, CUPCAKES, SOCK   1962
Ink and watercolor, 6 × 8¾ *in.*
The artist, New York

Oldenburg was making small-scale studies of objects found in
the Store with a business card for the Store in mind. The intention
involved the projection of a glittering miscellany, like the jumbled,
cheap, bright prizes in a penny chewing-gum machine.

Glorious
60's plastic.

C. D. 1962

125 NOTEBOOK SKETCH—FIFTY-SEVENTH STREET 1962
Crayon, 11 × 8½ in.
The artist, New York

In 1962 Oldenburg was invited to spend the summer working on a show for the Green Gallery on 57th Street. The drawing is a visualization of the sidewalks of 57th Street as imagined by him before entering that environment.

126 SKETCH TOWARD A SOFT SCULPTURE IN THE FORM OF A GIANT MAN 1962
Crayon and watercolor, 11 × 13¾ in.
The artist, New York

The drawing represents parts of the "body" of a cloth man, a soft sculpture intended to be hung out of the window of the Green Gallery on 57th Street. In the drawing, the space is interior. Whenever Oldenburg represents interior space, he fills it with lines which are a metaphor for dust, conversation, smells, the nature of light in enclosure.

128 GIANT SOFT SCULPTURES VISUALIZED IN GREEN GALLERY—HAT AND SHIRT   1962
Crayon and watercolor, 11½×17½ in.
The artist, New York

A visualization of the Green Gallery with the giant objects
Oldenburg had planned to make for it. The possible response
of visitors to the objects is also shown. The man at lower
right is lifting the brim of the Giant Hat. The inscription at the
bottom reads "at the show." In the actual exhibition, a Giant
Hamburger was substituted; the Giant Hat was never made.

130 ORIGINAL FOR POSTER ANNOUNCING ONE-MAN SHOW AT GREEN GALLERY—
BIPLANE 1962
Crayon, 13⅞ × 16⅞ in.
Provenance : 4
Jonathan D. Scull, New York

Original drawing for the poster announcing Oldenburg's
one-man show of sculptures and drawings in September, 1962.
The biplane motif acknowledges the collaboration of the artist's
wife in the making of the sculptures and "getting us aloft"
in their first uptown show. It is also a two-sexed image.

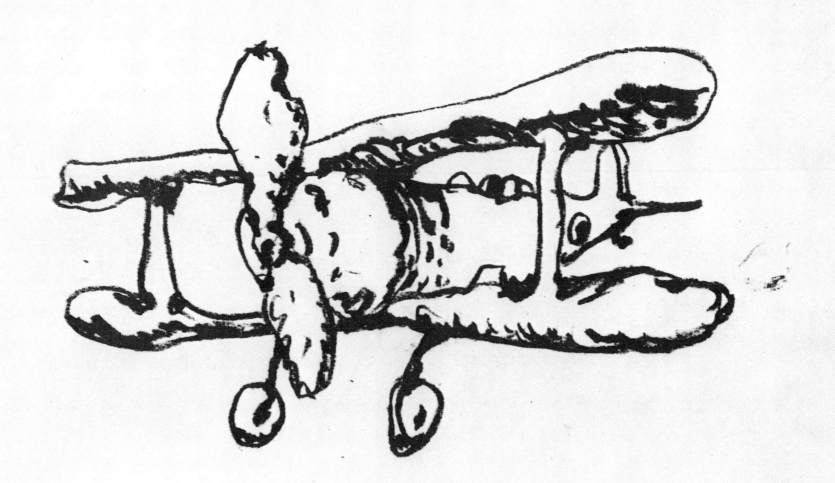

O. O. 62

132 CAKE WEDGE 1962
Crayon, 25 × 32⅜ in.
Provenance : 4
Collection of Mr. and Mrs. Robert C. Scull, New York

Oldenburg made this drawing from his sculpture, *Giant Cake Wedge*,
1962. This interpretation differs from the original in being open, linear,
light. The style of the drawing emphasizes a tendril-like development
of the form, as opposed to the voluminous style of the sculpture.

141 NOTEBOOK SKETCH—SILK SUMMER SHIRT 1963
Crayon, pencil, and watercolor, 7⅞ × 5⅜ in., mounted on sheet 11 × 8½ in.
The artist, New York

A sketch for a silk shirt made from souvenir scarves
of Washington, D.C. The shirt was later sewn
by the artist's wife and presented to Andy Warhol.

silk ~~~~~~~

NY 1967

142 NOTEBOOK SKETCH—MATERIAL AND SCISSORS 1963
Ink and watercolor, 11 × 8 ½ in.
The artist, New York

A sketch for a sculpture not yet executed. The conception
here is that material and scissors are unified.

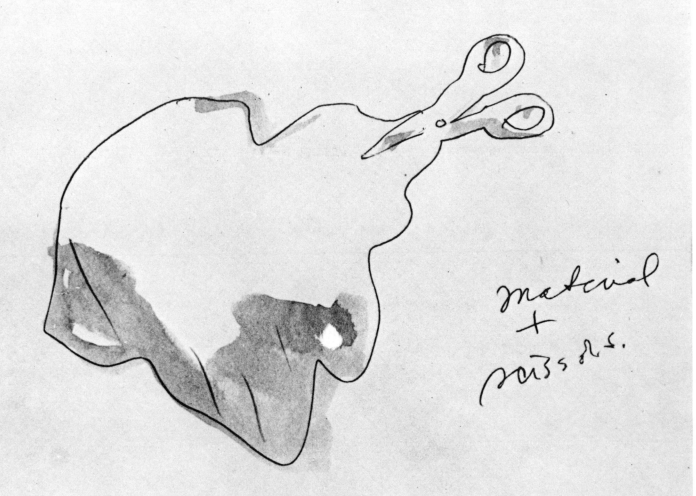

material
+
scissors.

143 NOTEBOOK SKETCH—POOL TABLE 1963
Ink, 11 × 8 ½ in.
The artist, New York

A sketch toward a sculpture based upon a pool table. The
idea was modified and finally realized as a ping-pong table.

pool Table

152 CIGARETTE WITH SOLID SMOKE AND SHAVING BRUSH 1963
Crayon and watercolor, 11 × 14 in.
The artist, New York

This is one of the drawings done in 1963 in transition between
the objects of the Store, in which color was emphasized, and
the objects of the Home, in which volume was emphasized.
This drawing served as the sketch for a small sculpture. It
contains a favorite device, the making tangible of an intangible
thing. Rendering the smoke as a solid is comparable to the
use of balloons of verbal expression in comic strips.

153   STUDY FOR SOFT TYPEWRITER   1963
Crayon and watercolor, 11½ × 13⅝ *in.*
Mr. and Mrs. Peter J. Solomon, New York

The telephone, the typewriter, and the fan have been Oldenburg's
favorite office subjects. Conceived as soft sculptures, they were
translated into black vinyl; to a degree the sculptural material imposed
itself on the forms. In the imaginative drawings leading to these
works, concept was more an issue of style. Style harmonized the various
formal associations with the effect Oldenburg was after. In the present
drawing, the typewriter suggests a scallop shell, but it is also used to
explore the sense of inflation. The voluminous style of the handling
reconciles the image with Oldenburg's interest in the pneumatic state.
The word "Busch" at the bottom of the drawing is a reference
to William Busch, the cartoonist who drew the Katzenjammer Kids.
Orphan Annie was another association. These cartoons were drawn
in a round style, involving balloon-like volume.

164 STUDY FOR ANNOUNCEMENT FOR ONE-MAN SHOW AT DWAN GALLERY—
MICKEY MOUSE WITH RED HEART 1963
Crayon and watercolor, 17×14 *in.*
Provenance : 5
Private collection, New York

Done in California as a sketch for a poster for an Oldenburg
exhibition held in Los Angeles in October, 1963. "The mouse is not
only Mickey Mouse, but an amalgam—the legion of American
movie mouse heroes." The heart comes from the plastic heart advertising sign of a chain of filling stations in the Los Angeles area.

168 STUDY FOR ANNOUNCEMENT FOR ONE-MAN SHOW AT DWAN GALLERY—
GOOD HUMOR ICE CREAM BAR 1963
Crayon and watercolor, 17×14 in.
The artist, New York

This is a poster study for the Dwan Gallery show held in Los Angeles
in October, 1963. The drawing is from Oldenburg's sculpture, *Giant
Good Humor*, made earlier in 1963. The white area toward the bottom
represents the bite taken out of the Good Humor, conventionally
shown in advertisements of the subject. In this drawing, as in many
others, Oldenburg's initials are included in the calligraphy.

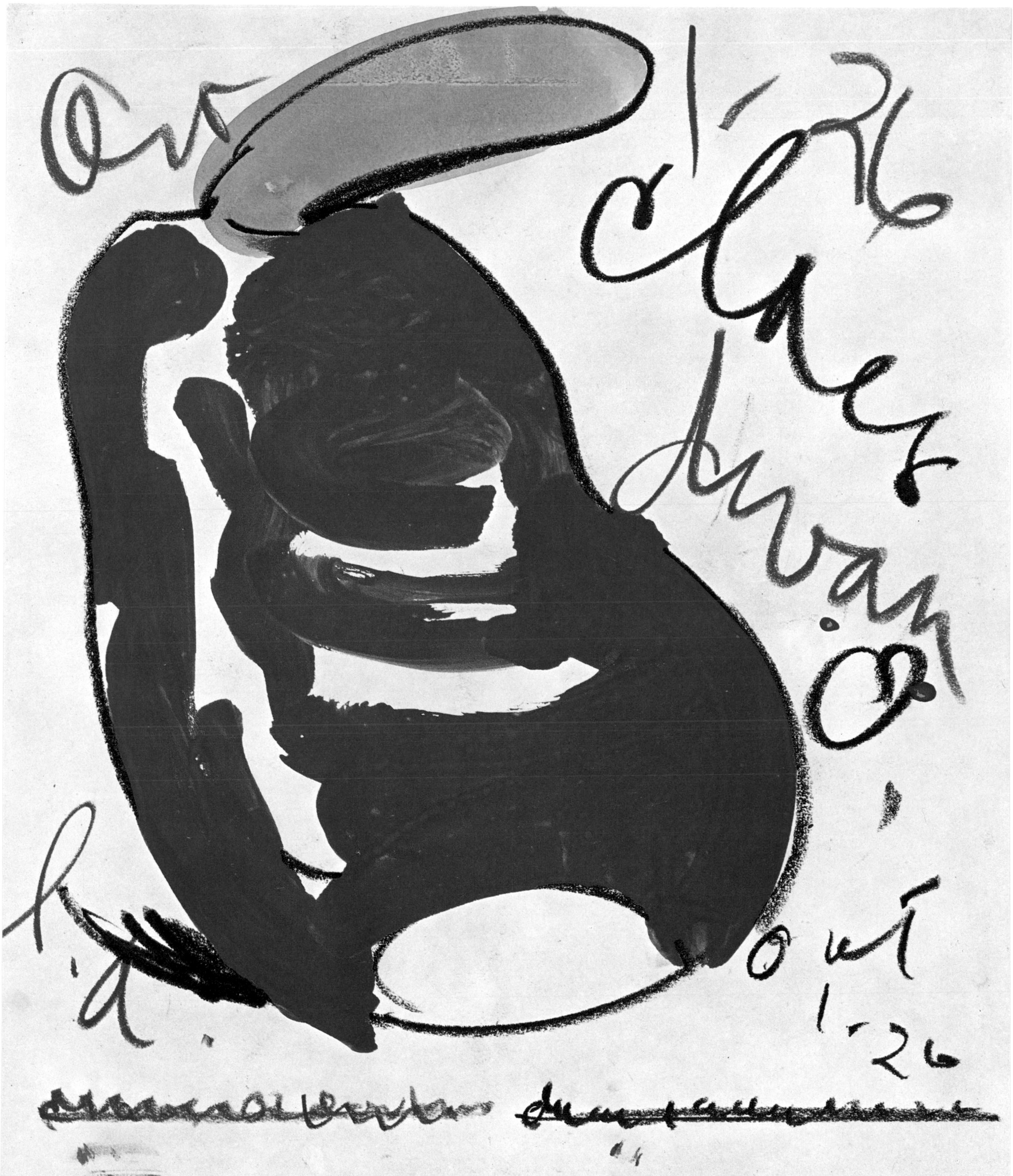
Oui
Oui
1.26

170 VISUALIZATION OF A GIANT SOFT SCULPTURE IN THE FORM OF A SHIRT
WITH TIE 1963
Crayon and watercolor, 14×16½ *in.*
Provenance : 2
Collection of Mr. and Mrs. Michael Blankfort, Los Angeles, California

Another imagined installation, with observer.

171 GIANT KITCHEN CHAIR ON ITS SIDE—CHROME-HOME 1963
Crayon and watercolor, 13 ⅞ × 16 ⅝ in.
The artist, New York

This drawing was done in the period of the Home objects. The chair is visualized as a giant sculpture in a gallery space. "Chrome-Home" both refers to the incidence of chrome in the home situation and echoes the form of the chair, which itself makes, as seen on its side, a rectangular CO, Oldenburg's initials.

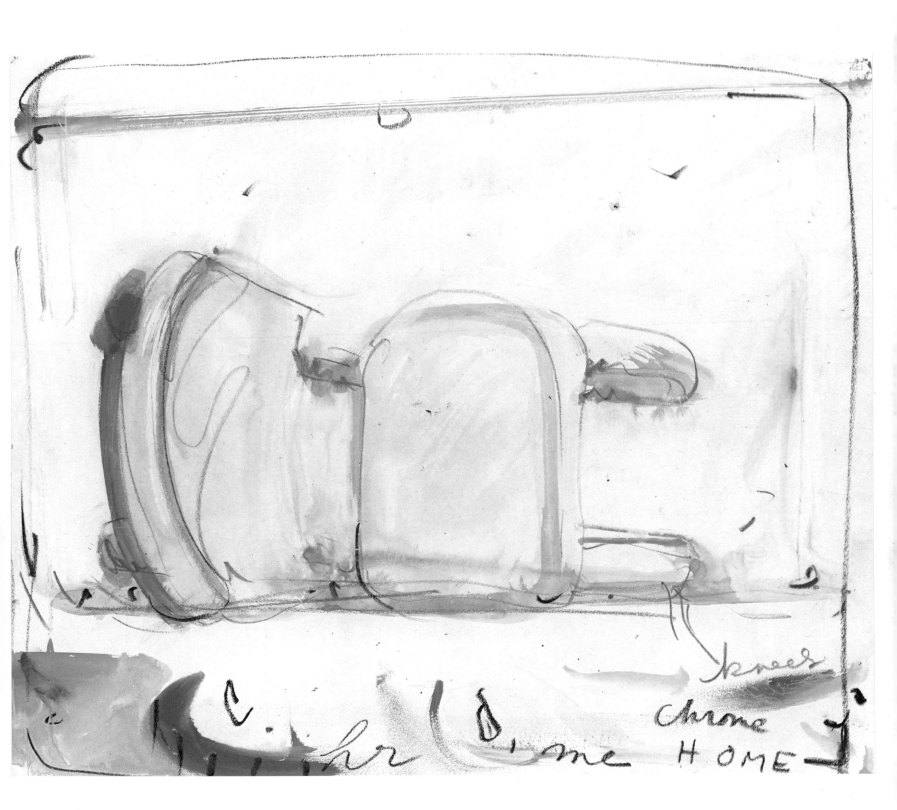

knees

C.hr d me chrome
HOME

175 STUDY FOR A POSTER FOR "4 ENVIRONMENTS," SIDNEY JANIS GALLERY—
THE HOME 1963
Crayon and watercolor, 24 × 18 *in.*
Provenance : 5 ; Paul Bianchini, New York
The Joan and Lester Avnet Collection, New York

Sketch for a poster advertising the *Bedroom Ensemble*, first
shown in January, 1964, at the Sidney Janis Gallery. Oldenburg
had gone to Los Angeles to break the patterns of his life
and work in New York. He returned briefly in January with
this announcement of his new-found interests. The calligraphy
reflects a shift in concern from line to volume.

176 STUDY OF BED WITH BEDTABLES—BEDROOM ENSEMBLE 1963
Chalk and spray enamel, 26½ × 41 in.
Provenance : 3
Dr. Hubert Peeters Van Hoorenbeeck, Bruges, Belgium

The *Bedroom Ensemble* was the first large statement of the
Home period, when Oldenburg's interest shifted to the
use of domestic objects as metaphors for the concerns of
sculpture. He adopted a quasi-architectural rendering
style. The use of chalk on black paper suggests a blueprint.

6 FLYING PIZZA 1964

Color lithograph, 22 × 30 in.
Edition: 200
Printed by Irwin Hollander, New York
Publisher: Tanglewood Press, New York
Signed Claes Oldenburg in full in pencil at the bottom right and numbered from 1 to 200

Pies have always interested Oldenburg; he associates them with the performance of a cross section. The cross section yields two dominant views of the object, an elevation and an interior. Oldenburg takes satisfaction in a visual convention that discovers at the same time and in the same form as it expresses. The cross section meets a need of his obsessive curiosity even as it provides him with a means to convey his discovery. In this drawing, the pizza is set on its end. The impossibility of setting a pizza on end in reality intensifies the sensation of softness in the drawn forms. The pizza sections "are behaving like sheep jumping over an obstacle"—as perhaps in "counting sheep." At the same time, the forms are looming. The turn in the pastry is made to seem a threatening cornice.

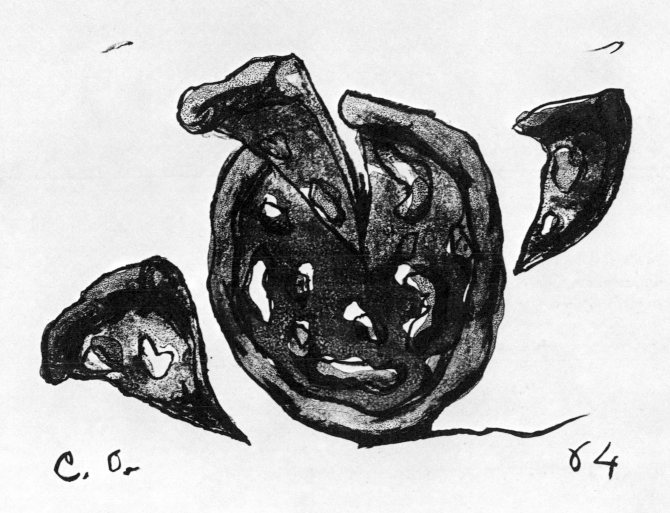

C. Or   64

185 STUDY FOR A SCULPTURE IN THE FORM OF A PING-PONG TABLE 1964
Chalk, collage, and watercolor, 26½ × 41 in.
Provenance : 5 ; Collection Buckwalter, Kansas City, Missouri ; Paul Bianchini, New York;
Dwan Gallery, New York
Dr. and Mrs. Judd Marmor, Los Angeles, California

Another drawing in the industrial style. The chalk line takes on an
electric luminosity in the darkened, constricted "home" space. At one
stage of the drawing, Oldenburg was undecided whether to draw a pool
table or a ping-pong table; evidence of this uncertainty remains in the
left hand section. The space in this drawing, while interior, also reflects
a concept of limitless outer darkness, in contrast to the drawings which
involve the white-light space of the earth's atmosphere. The luminous
ping-pong balls scattered on the floor become stars and planets.

188 PLAN FOR A SCULPTURE IN THE FORM OF WALL SWITCHES 1964
Ink and watercolor, 28⅝ × 23⅜ in.
Provenance : 5
Whitney Museum of American Art, New York, Neysa McMein Purchase Award

This drawing is essentially a guide to the carpenter. The present
version is taken a bit further because it appeared on the cover
of Oldenburg's 1964 exhibition catalogue. It is an example of a technical
drawing carried into the decorative. Part of it is a rubbing of an
actual switch from a bungalow in Venice, California. An element in
Oldenburg's treatment of the subject was his recollection of
"the deep, dark windows in drawings of visionary architecture."

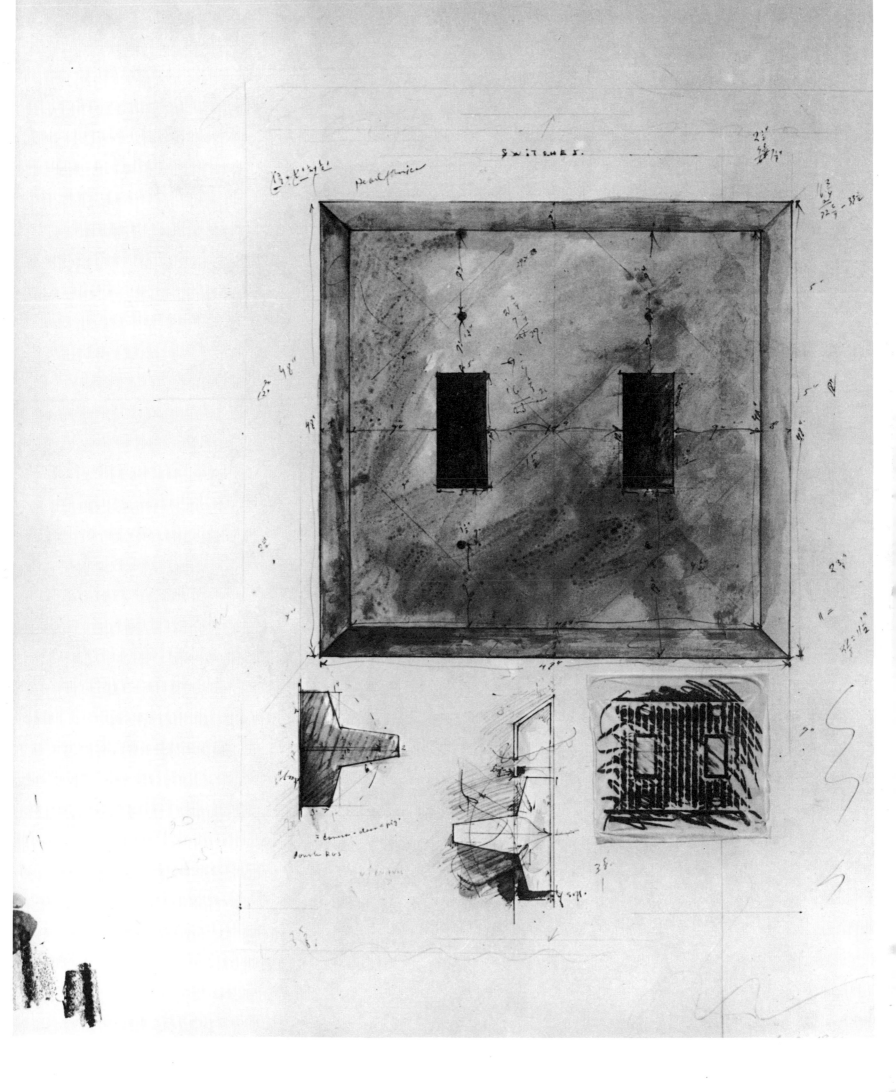

192   STUDY FOR A SCULPTURE IN THE FORM OF A VACUUM CLEANER—FROM SIDE 1964
Chalk and watercolor, 40×26 in.
Provenance : 3
Dr. Hubert Peeters Van Hoorenbeeck, Bruges, Belgium

Sketch for a sculpture using the elements of a vacuum cleaner, in imitation
of industrial style. As Oldenburg had earlier identified himself with the
makers of street graffiti in order to mimic their style in his own terms
imaginatively, he now identified with the industrial designer to get close
to the feel of another technique and discipline. In doing these pieces,
he was deliberately putting obstacles in the way of direct expression.
The necessary intervention of craftsmen in the realization of sculptures
of this type was another form of removal and interference.

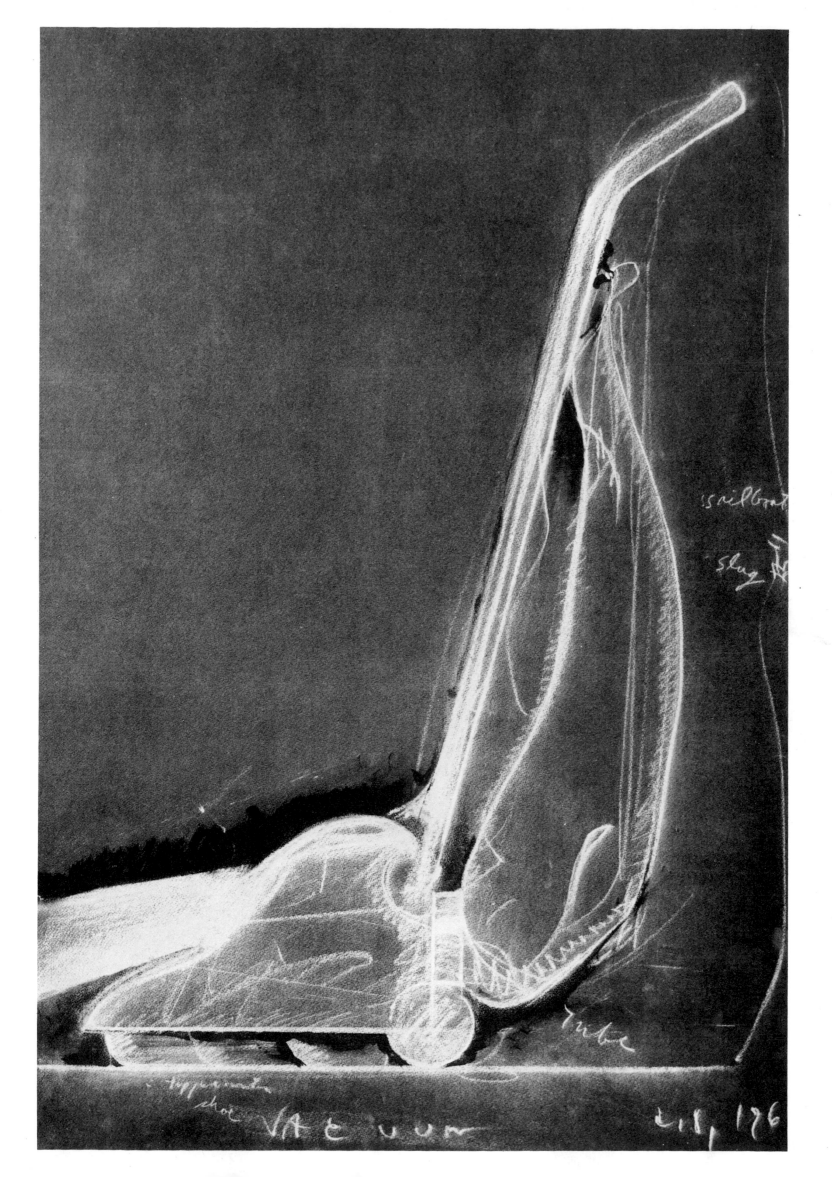

194 STUDY FOR A SOFT SCULPTURE IN THE FORM OF A TOASTER 1964
Crayon and watercolor, 11½×13½ in.
Provenance: 5; Leon Kraushar, New York; Karl Ströher, Darmstadt, West Germany
Private collection, New York

A drawing exploiting the roundness of the metal object, so that
the sensation of the bulging form is dominant both formally and
expressively. The holes suggest the holes in the light switches.

206 PROPOSED COLOSSAL MONUMENT FOR THE BATTERY, N.Y.C.—VACUUM CLEANER,
VIEW FROM THE UPPER BAY 1965
Crayon and watercolor, 23 × 29 in.
Provenance : 5
Jonathan D. Scull, New York

An early monument. "At this period, the vision was of throwing an
enlarged version of one of my objects onto the face of New York. This
was an attempt to represent my objects in a new scale."

N.41   C.8.6i

209 PROPOSED COLOSSAL MONUMENT FOR GRAND ARMY PLAZA, N.Y.C.—
BAKED POTATO 1965
Crayon and watercolor, 18 × 21¼ in.
Provenance : 5
Collection of Mr. and Mrs. Ira Licht, New York

"The first suggestion of a monument came some years ago as I was
riding in from the airport. I thought: how nice it would be to have a
large rabbit about the size of a skyscraper in midtown. It would cheer
people up seeing its ears from the suburbs. The spot I had in mind was
the space in front of the Plaza Hotel (where there is already a fountain).
However, the Playboy Club later made its headquarters nearby which
made construction of the giant rabbit at that particular spot impossible.
I substituted the baked potato, in either of two versions: upright or
thrown against the wall of the hotel."

B.P. in
grand Plaza

216 PROPOSED COLOSSAL MONUMENT FOR LOWER EAST SIDE—IRONING BOARD 1965
Crayon and watercolor, 21¾ × 29½ in.
Provenance : 5
Mr. and Mrs. Marvin Goodman, Toronto, Canada

The ironing board with iron, which had been realized
as sculpture, is here placed on the Lower East Side of the
island of Manhattan, whose shape it echoes. The top of the
board is envisaged as a helicopter landing platform.

n.y.

C. Iou 1865

232 PROPOSED MONUMENT FOR THE INTERSECTION OF CANAL STREET AND
BROADWAY, N.Y.C.—BLOCK OF CONCRETE INSCRIBED WITH THE NAMES
OF WAR HEROES 1965
Crayon and watercolor, 15⅞ × 12 in.
Provenance : 5
Collection of Alicia Legg, New York

One of several drawings projecting the placement of a colossal
cube of concrete to seal the intersection. In the monument series,
the emphasis is heavily upon the concept. Sometimes the
drawing is a bare indication in order to stimulate the imagination,
as in this example. The impressionistic treatment, derived
from his earlier landscape style, is used as if Oldenburg
were at the site. He has rendered the imaginary as actual.

236 PROPOSED COLOSSAL MONUMENT FOR PARK AVENUE, N.Y.C.—
GOOD HUMOR BAR 1965
Crayon and watercolor, 23½ × 17½ in.
Provenance : 5
Carroll Janis, New York

One of the first of the colossal monuments, in effect,
a softening of the Pan Am Building. The bite out
of the ice cream bar is the roadway through.

238 STUDY FOR A SCREENPRINT IN THE FORM OF A PIZZA—PIZZA COMPONENTS
(not executed)
Crayon and watercolor, 16⅝ × 14 in.
The artist, New York

"After eating a pizza, I made a recollected study of the solids:
the paper became the medium of the cheese. I mention this because
the paper is never merely itself in my drawing but is always a
metaphor for some character of space." Every drawing has also a
calligraphic element which is separate from representation; in
this instance, Oldenburg discovered afterward that the mushrooms
had gone in the direction of skulls, and the result seems less a
depiction of pizza than a free statement in the language of drawing.

251 SKETCH OF A 3-WAY PLUG 1965
Crayon and oil wash, 30½ × 23 in.
Provenance : 5
Sam J. Wagstaff, Jr., Detroit, Michigan

The first sketch in the 3-way plug series—a rapid, painterly treatment in contrast to the detailed architectural drawings which followed, leading to the large paper sculpture.

c18. '65

256   BLUE TOILET   1965
Collage, crayon and watercolor, 29¾ × 21¾ in.
Provenance : 3
Dr. Hubert Peeters Van Hoorenbeeck, Bruges, Belgium

Along with the functional drawings for sculpture of this period,
Oldenburg was doing expressive and impressionistic drawings
visualizing the appearance of the projected sculpture.

257 STUDY OF A DORMEYER MIXER 1965
Pencil, 30×22³/₁₆ in.
Provenance : 5
Emily S. Rauh, St. Louis, Missouri

Elaborations upon a technical drawing for the soft sculpture *Dormeyer Mixer*, 1965-1966. After the drawing was used to make patterns for the sculpture, Oldenburg returned to it and developed the metamorphic and fantastic elements of the subject. The cord was added and compared with renderings of trees in the drawings of Corot. Ovals, suggestive of windows, were added to the revolving unit of the mixer, producing the impression of a cathedral dome. The grip was hatched; the form reminded the artist of an ibex horn. The upper right hand corner contains notations—common in Oldenburg's drawings—relating the subject to another object in his production, in this case, the Iron.

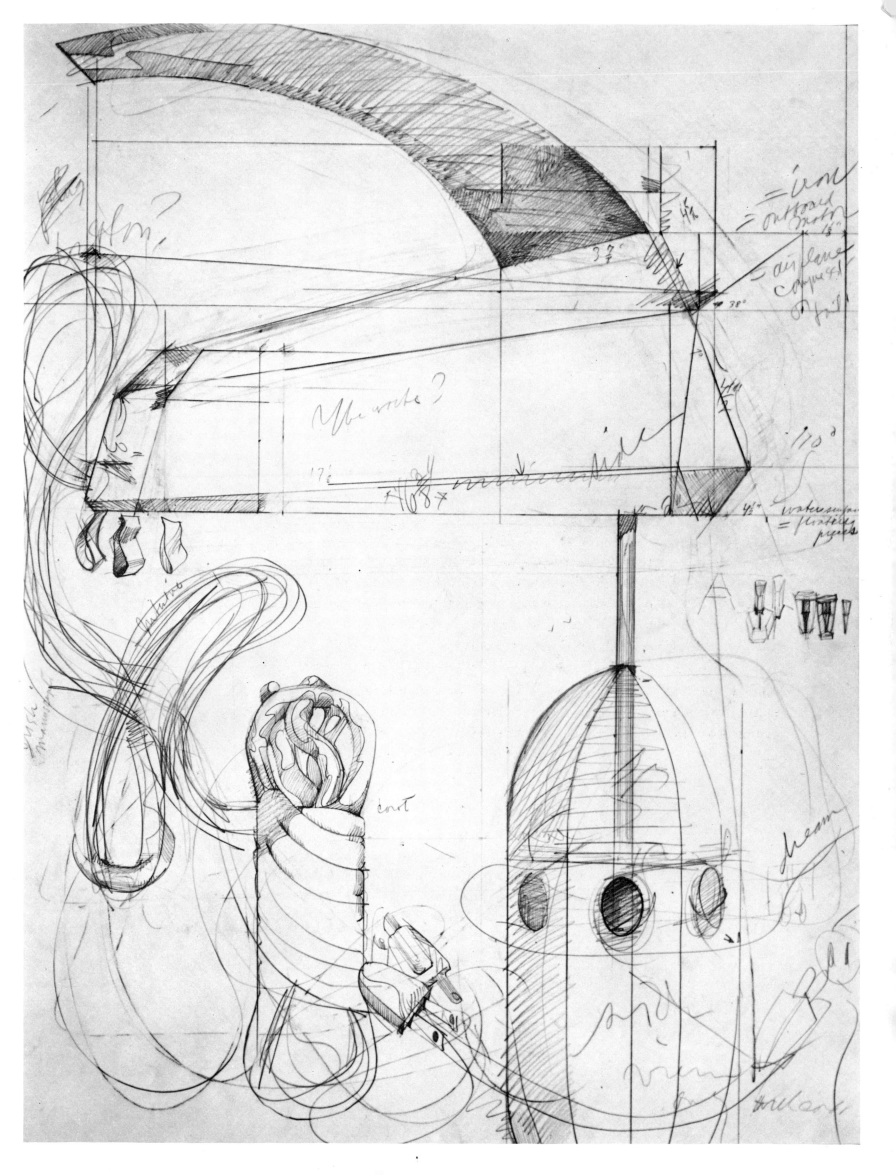

258 PROFILE STUDY OF THE AIRFLOW 1965
Collage, pencil, and watercolor, 22 × 29¾ in.
Provenance : 5
Harry N. Abrams Family Collection, New York

This is the first attempt to create a drawn version of the Airflow automobile from photographs and snapshots. The corrections were executed on layers of tracing paper. The drawing was enlarged by photoprinting to the full size of the car and was used to make patterns for soft sculptures based upon parts of the Airflow: the doors, the tires, and the rear assembly.

from C-17, 1937.   Oct 1965   Study of Claes Oldenburg

259 SKETCH OF THE AIRFLOW, FROM A SNAPSHOT (FRONT END) 1965
Crayon, 30×22 in.
Provenance : 5
Collection of John and Kimiko Powers, Aspen, Colorado

The first drawing in the Airflow series based upon a color snapshot
of the car. "I wanted the subject to materialize slowly, to be an
apparition—a surprise—and so reduced the clear detail of the snapshot
to a vaporous, pale rendering." The crayon was crushed and the line
was broken by placing rough cardboard under the smooth paper during
the execution. Oldenburg then muted the colors with silver crayon.

graphite study - Auto

C. O. 1965

263   THE AIRFLOW—TOP AND BOTTOM, FRONT, BACK, SIDES, WITH SILHOUETTE
      OF THE INVENTOR   1965
      Collage with pen and spray enamel, 17½ × 17¾ in.
      Provenance : 5
      The 180 Beacon Collection of Contemporary Art, Boston, Massachusetts

The original of a cover made for *Art News*, intended to be folded into
a box showing all views of the automobile. The silhouette is drawn
from a snapshot of the car's inventor, Carl Breer. The drawing is com-
posed of many separate parts, glued together slightly out of register.

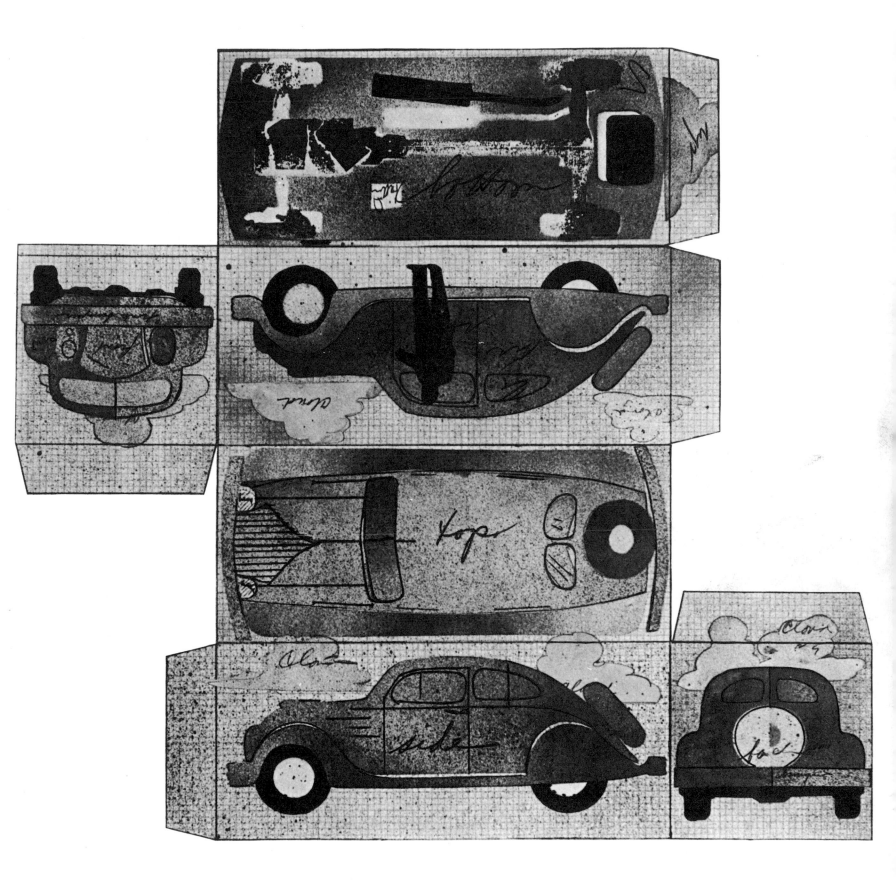

267 PATTERNS USED IN THE SEWING OF THE SOFT RADIATOR, FAN AND FANBELT—
THE AIRFLOW 1966
Cut-outs, felt pen, and spray enamel, 40 x 26 in.
The artist, New York

A preoccupation of Oldenburg's is the lifting of the image out of
its environment. This, of course, is an inevitable step in the preparation
of patterns for sculpture; but it has its equivalent in the imaginative
drawings that are torn or cut out. The projection of the image as object
enhances its formal quality. So to speak, the internal relationships,
create the surrounding space. Often the patterns, while practical, are
also strong enough to transform themselves into presences.

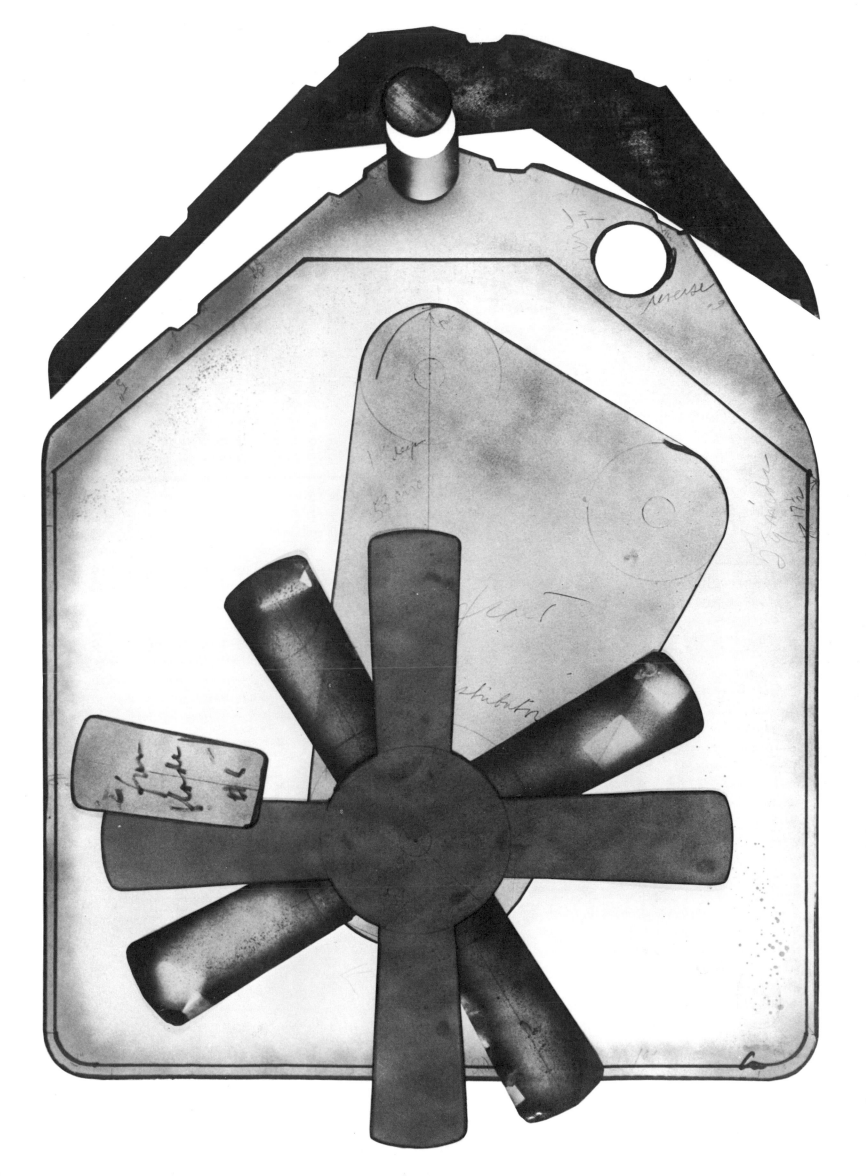

268 PATTERN USED IN THE SEWING OF THE SOFT TRANSMISSION BOX—
THE AIRFLOW 1966
Cut-out drawing, pencil, and spray enamel, 25 ½ × 40 in.

Patterns such as this are a necessary preliminary to the making
of all soft sculpture, which is sewn. Expression here is
subordinated to function. The shapes are arrived at through
a rigorous and practical simplification of the original objects.

270 STUDY OF A 3-WAY PLUG CUBE TAP—SKETCH FOR A POSTER *(not executed)* 1966
Pencil, 40×26 in.
Provenance: 5
Art Institute of Chicago, Chicago, Illinois, Restricted Gift of The Blum-Kovler Foundation

A meticulous rendering in perspective, whose chief purpose was to
facilitate the construction of the sculpture. Oldenburg worked from an
actual plug but altered, even idealized, the proportions of the object.
The roughed-in lettering is an attempt to adapt the drawing to an
announcement for the artist's 1966 exhibition at the Sidney Janis Gallery.

276 FALLING TEA BAG 1966
Crayon and watercolor, 6⅛ × 4¼ in.
The artist, New York

One of several drawings visualizing an object being dropped,
in this case seen just before it strikes the ground. An earlier conception, the multiple *Teabag*, 1965, shows the object after impact.

280   STUDY OF A SWEDISH BREAD—KNÄCKEBRÖD *(for a multiple in cast iron)*   1966
Pencil and watercolor, 24 × 21 in.
Provenance: 5
Collection of Max Kozloff, New York

Analysis of common Swedish hardbread, toward
realization of a multiple in 250 copies, cast in iron and
rusted, a gift to the Stockholm Moderna Museet at the
time of Oldenburg's one-man show there, October, 1966.

306 FAG END 1966
Crayon and watercolor, 15 × 22 in.
The artist, New York

In London in 1966, Oldenburg collected cigarette butts as one might collect butterflies, interested in the different shapes they took in being stamped out after use. Treating the butts from the viewpoint of sculpture, he made studies of them in different scales. The present drawing imagines a colossal butt to be placed in Hyde Park.

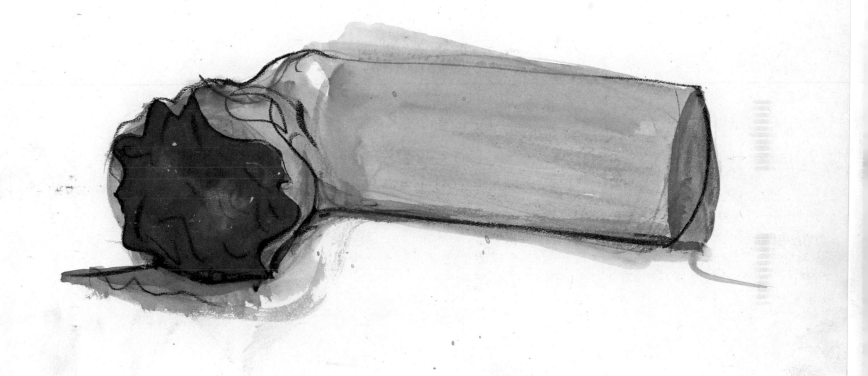

dagval   EA 66

308 LIGHT SWITCHES, LONDON 1966
Crayon and watercolor, 9½×7 in.
The artist, New York

In London, Oldenburg conceived of a multiple consisting of a slice
of English wallpaper on which an unconnected English wall switch
was to be attached magnetically, so that it might be moved about.
English wallpaper made him recall the furniture and wallpaper
fantasies of Ensor, and he recorded Ensor's name in the drawing.

315 BASE OF COLOSSAL DRAINPIPE MONUMENT (TORONTO) WITH WATERFALL 1967
Pencil and watercolor, 24¾ × 22 in.
Provenance : 5
Collection of John and Kimiko Powers, Aspen, Colorado

A monument proposed for the shoreline of Toronto, intended to
rise 850 feet in a T shape and to contain a water supply that empties
in a waterfall at the base sited between public recreation areas.

317 PROPOSED COLOSSAL UNDERGROUND MONUMENT—DRAINPIPE 1967
Cut-out, pencil, spray enamel, and watercolor, 40×26 in.
Provenance : 5
Mr. and Mrs. M. Riklis, New York

One of a series of concealed monuments, in which only the
exterior is meant to be seen. The drainpipe interior is to be viewed
through a small hole, the size of a golf cup. The viewer is to lie
facing downward in the center of an acre of well-tended grass.

The drawing is a cut-out. Oldenburg wanted the sense of a machined,
metallic edge, isolated from the surrounding material. The drawing was
sprayed; Oldenburg cut it in order to make the edge precise.

Color plate courtesy M. Riklis

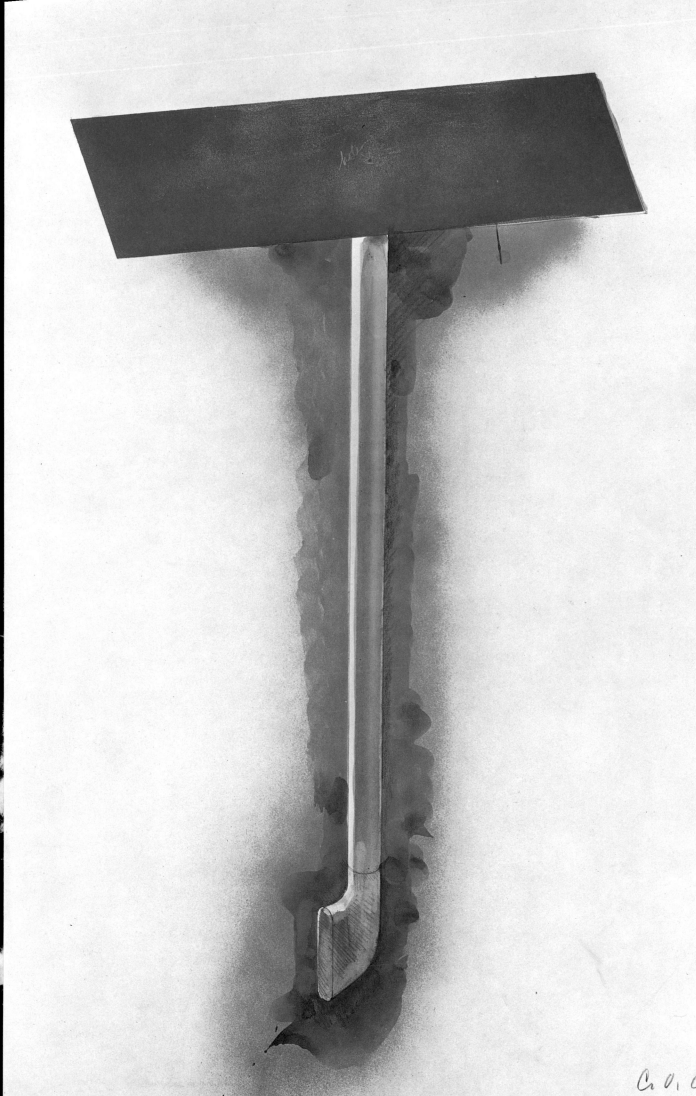

323 SMALL MONUMENT FOR A LONDON STREET—FALLEN HAT (FOR
     ADLAI STEVENSON) 1967
     Crayon, 15 ½ × 22 in.
     Collection of John and Kimiko Powers, Aspen, Colorado

This monument derives from two sources, the death of a friend
on the street and the death of Adlai Stevenson on a London
Street. The monument is intended for bronze and to be one
of the "obstacle" monuments on a small scale to be set into
a London paving stone, so that passersby might trip over it.

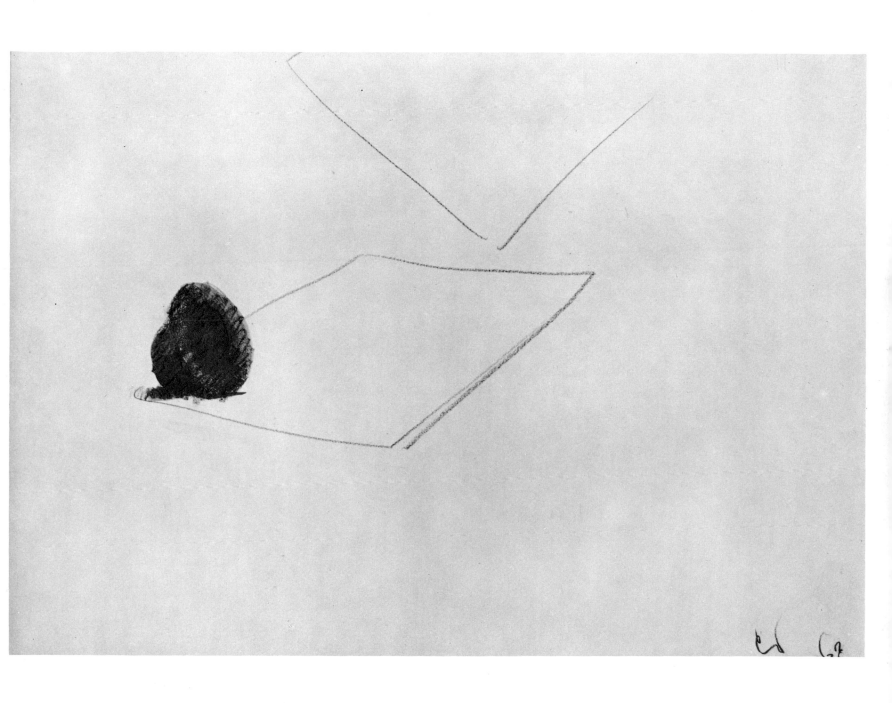

326 PROPOSED COLOSSAL MONUMENT FOR THAMES RIVER—THAMES BALL COCK 1967
Crayon, pen, and watercolor on postcard, 3½ × 5½ in.
Provenance: 5
Carroll Janis, New York

Giant copper ball for the Thames River based on a copper ball toilet
float, suggested by the similarity of the tidal flow to the emptying
and refilling of the cistern. The float monument would be buoyant
and brilliant and would supply Londoners with the sun.

329 PROPOSED COLOSSAL MONUMENT—FAN IN PLACE OF THE STATUE OF LIBERTY,
BEDLOES ISLAND 1967
Pencil, 26×40 in.
Provenance : 5
Steve Schapiro, New York

A monument that exploits similarity of form. The base of the fan echoes
the base of the Statue of Liberty. There are other similarities, such as
the crown and the implied circumstance of the wind blowing up the bay.

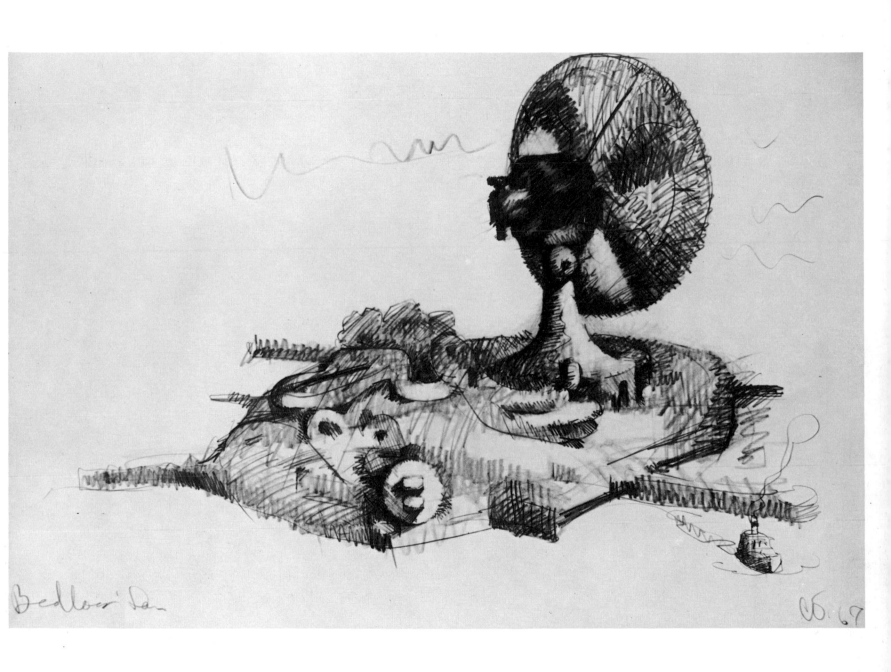

Bedloss Dan   CO.68

333 COLOSSAL FAG ENDS IN PARK SETTING, WITH MAN 1967
Pencil and watercolor, 30×22 in.
Provenance : 5
Mrs. René d'Harnoncourt, New York

Oldenburg developed a style of naturalistic rendering in connection
with his monument series. It was necessary for him to project the
image of what he wanted as if it were already there, but the demands
of drawing required something more; the style is the resolution of this
problem. The early monument drawings are more impressionistic.
At the time the present drawing was made, Oldenburg had moved
toward a more photographic rendering. He had become almost
perversely interested in realistic Victorian draftsmanship, and this
is an influence. The site is Hyde Park.

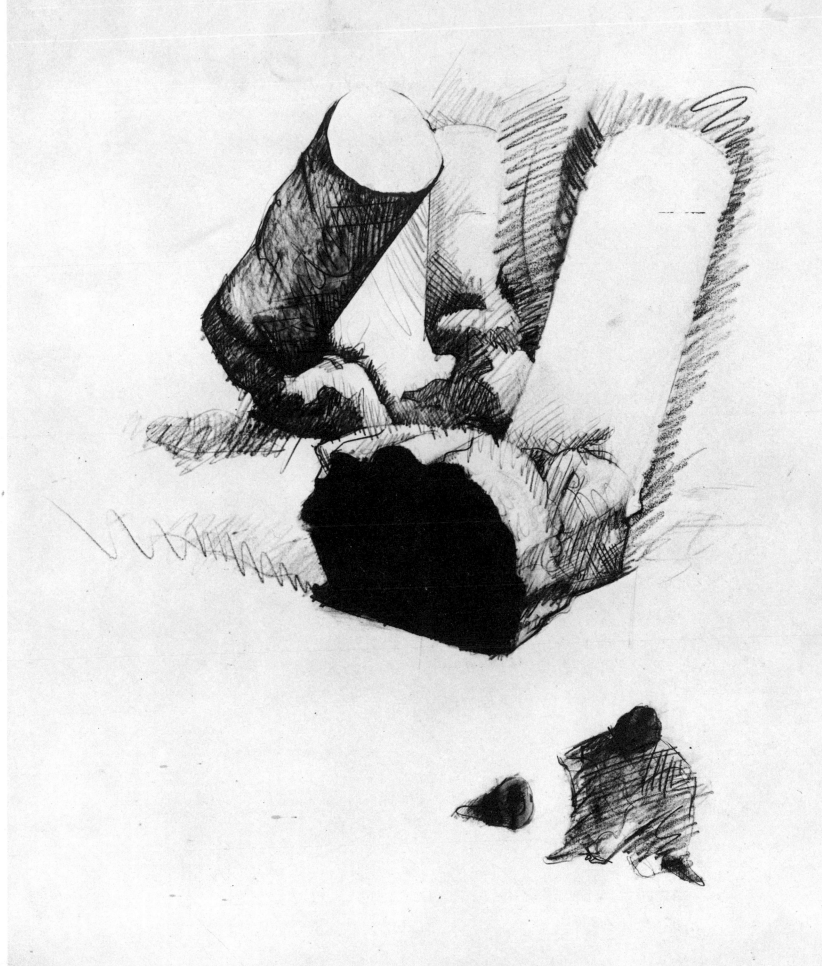

Long Ends in Park
w. man   s. 62

334 FAG ENDS IN BAG ASH TRAY 1967
Crayon and watercolor, 30×22 in.
Provenance : 5
Mr. and Mrs. Seymour Propp, New York

Sketch for a projected sculpture utilizing a cloth-based ash tray.
In functional drawings such as this one, the space surrounding
the object is relatively neutral. The emphasis is in rendering
the object as it will look. This drawing is more involved with
natural than with imaginative change. The style is naturalistic.

Soft Ash Tray   CW 69

348 DROPPED CUP OF COFFEE—STUDY FOR *Image of the Buddha Preaching*
BY FRANK O'HARA 1967
Pencil and watercolor, 30×22 in.
Museum of Modern Art, New York, Gift of the artist

One of several attempts to illustrate a poem by Frank O'Hara
for a collection issued after O'Hara's death. The illustration
was for one of the Lunch poems; this drawing combines a
representation of the manner of his death with the circumstances
of the writing of the poem. (Another illustration was used.)

349 STRIPPER WITH BATTLESHIP—STUDY FOR *Image of the Buddha Preaching*
BY FRANK O'HARA 1967
Pencil, 30×22 in.
Museum of Modern Art, New York, Gift of Mr. and Mrs. Richard E. Oldenburg

This is one of several preparatory drawings for Oldenburg's
contribution to the Frank O'Hara memorial volume published
by the Museum of Modern Art. It is the last of the erotic
naturalistic drawings done by Oldenburg in the spring of 1967.
The poem it illustrates is concerned with Indian and German
culture. In this drawing, Indian culture is represented by a stripper
and German culture by a garment in the form of a battleship.

With his erotic drawings, Oldenburg returned to the figure.
He emphasized a sharp, hard line, using, in general, ballpoint pen or pencil. He had in mind early 19th century
draftsmanship, a balance of classical and romantic elements.

351 STUDY FOR THE GIANT SOFT DRUM SET 1967
Pencil and spray enamel, 30×22 in.
Provenance : 5
Collection of John and Kimiko Powers, Aspen, Colorado

Oldenburg began working on studies for the *Soft Drum Set* before a summer trip to Aspen, Colorado. Once there, he recognized certain affinities between his conception and the appearance of the landscape. In further studies, he emphasized these coincident qualities. This is one of the pre-Aspen drawings, an anticipation of the Aspen landscape.

352 DRUM PEDAL STUDY—FROM A SLINGERLAND DRUM CATALOGUE 1967
Pencil, 30×22 in.
Provenance : 5
Collection of John and Kimiko Powers, Aspen, Colorado

Based upon a catalogue illustration, and the first step
in simplifying an actual drum pedal in order to realize it
as part of the sculpture, *Giant Soft Drum Set*, 1967.

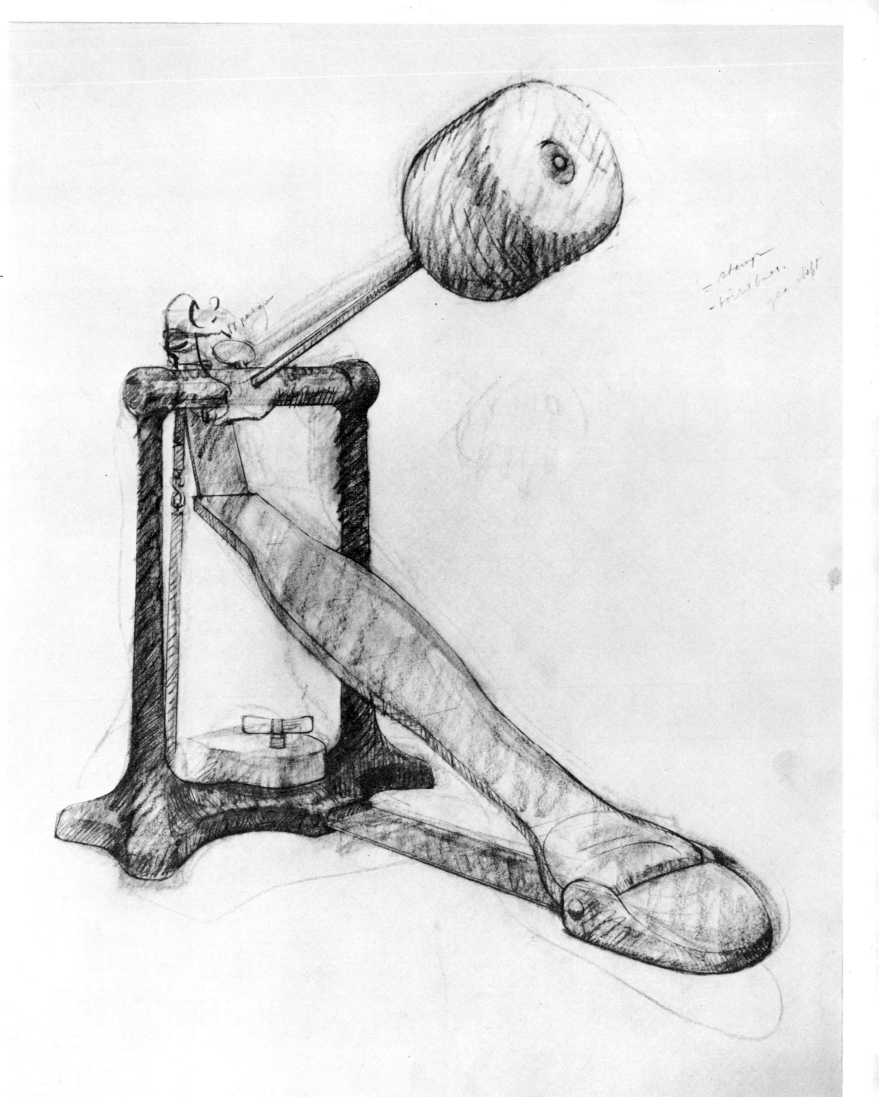

CW 67

353 DRUM PEDAL STUDY—SCHEMATIC RENDERING 1967
Pencil and watercolor, 30×22 in.
Provenance : 5
Collection of John and Kimiko Powers, Aspen, Colorado

Simplification of a drum pedal derived from a Slingerland drum
catalogue, in preparation for the *Collapsed Pedal* sculpture of the *Soft
Drum Set*. The treatment here suggested a later adaptation of the
pedal form: a projected hilltop monument for Aspen, Colorado, where
the pedal rises against the sky, as against a drum hide.

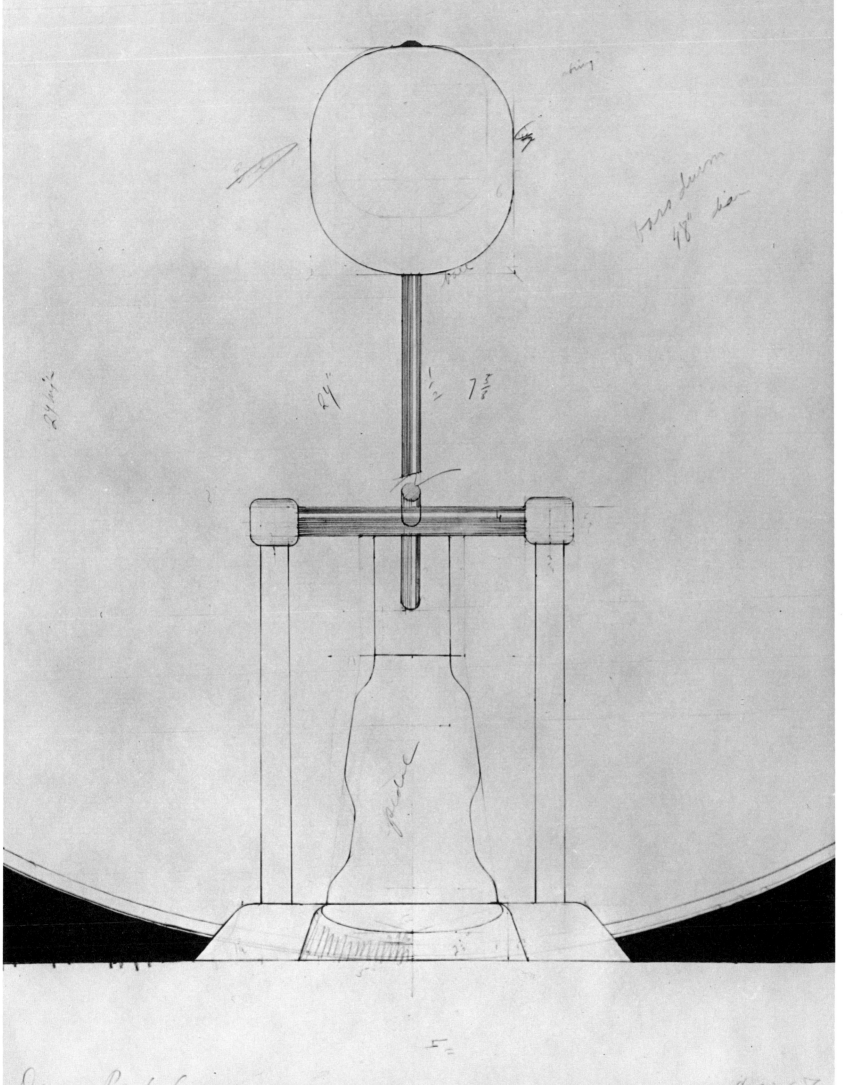

Drum Pedal

354 DRUM PEDAL STUDY—VISUALIZATION OF COLLAPSED VERSION 1967
Pencil, 30×22 in.
Provenance : 5
Collection of John and Kimiko Powers, Aspen, Colorado

An imagined version of the drum pedal structure in
collapse, intensified by Oldenburg's reading in de Sade at
the time and also, particularly, of Peter Weiss's *Investigation*.

363 PROPOSED COLOSSAL MONUMENT FOR THE WEST SIDE OF CHICAGO IN THE FORM
OF SMOKE 1967
Crayon and watercolor, 7 × 9¾ in.
The artist, New York

A sketch in terms of its subject. A rough accumulation of crayon
and color mimics the appearance of smoke, effects Oldenburg observed
while he was flying into Chicago. The monument envisages the
smoke cloud made solid and suspended unmoving above the city.

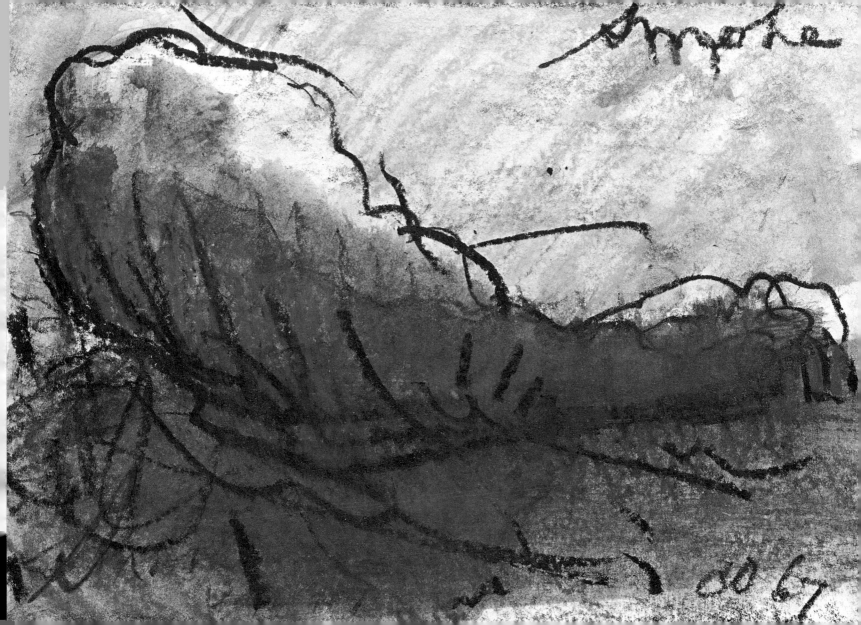

365 LATE SUBMISSION TO THE CHICAGO TRIBUNE ARCHITECTURAL COMPETITION
OF 1922—CLOTHESPIN, VERSION ONE 1967
Crayon, pencil, and watercolor, 22 × 23¼ in.
Provenance : 5
Philip Johnson, New Canaan, Connecticut

In subject the drawing represents a shift of interest to architecture,
emphasized by the image's location in a site famous in architectural
history. In order to obtain precision and miniaturism suggestive
of scale, Oldenburg used colored pencils for the first time. In graphic
terms, he set himself the problem of making a recognizable
clothespin seem convincingly as large as the Tribune Tower.

368 SCISSORS IN ACTION 1967
Collage and crayon, 30×20 *in.*
The artist, New York

An early study for a poster to commemorate the opening of the
new galleries of the National Collection of Fine Arts, Smithsonian
Institution, Washington, D.C. Oldenburg often uses the scissors as a
substitute for the pencil in creating line. He keeps several different
scissors which have individual cutting effects. Oldenburg had
made studies of the different shapes of these scissors; eventually the
shapes were combined into an ideal scissors which was proposed,
in colossal scale, as a substitute for the Washington Monument.

Chronology

1929	Born January 28, Stockholm, Sweden.
1930-31	Periods of residence in New York City and Rye, New York.
1933-37	Residence in Oslo, Norway.
1937-56	Residence in Chicago.
1946-50	Studied at Yale University. B.A. Degree in English and Art.
1950-52	Apprentice reporter, City News Bureau, Chicago.
1952-54	Night and day school studies, Art Institute of Chicago. Painting study with Paul Wieghardt.
1955-56	Studio in Chicago. Illustrations for *Chicago* magazine.
1956	Moved to New York City.
1956-61	Daily part-time job as library assistant at Cooper Union Museum Library.

1958

| December | First showing of drawings in New York City, at Red Grooms' City Gallery. |

1959

March	One-man show of drawings at Cooper Union Art School Library, New York City.
May	First one-man show of constructions in New York City at Judson Gallery.
July-August	Worked and showed in Lenox, Massachusetts.
November	Two-man show (with Jim Dine) at Judson Gallery.

1960

January-March	"Ray Gun" show. Environment and happening, "Snapshots from the City," at Judson Gallery.
January	"Below Zero," group show at Reuben Gallery, New York City.
May	One-man show, second version of "The Street," at Reuben Gallery. "New Media, New Forms I," at the Martha Jackson Gallery, New York City.
July-August	Worked in Provincetown, Massachusetts, and showed there at the Sun Gallery.
September	"New Media, New Forms II," Martha Jackson Gallery.
December	"Blackouts," happenings at the New Reuben Gallery.

1961

February	"Ironworks" and "Fotodeath," happenings at the New Reuben Gallery.
March	Constructions shown in three-man show at Alan Gallery, New York City.
May	"The Store," first version, in "Environments, Situations, Spaces" at Martha Jackson Gallery.
September	Group show at Green Gallery, New York City.
October	"Recent Acquisitions" at the Museum of Modern Art, New York City.
December	"The Store," second version, opened in a store at 107 East 2nd Street, New York City.

1962

January-May	"Ray Gun Theater," ten theater pieces at "The Store" on 2nd Street.
April	"The Store" transported to the Dallas Museum of Contemporary Art, Dallas, Texas.
April	"Injun," happening commissioned by the Dallas Museum of Contemporary Art.
June	"Pat's Birthday," film with Robert Breer.
September	One-man show at the Green Gallery.
October	"Sports," happening at the Green Gallery.
November	"New Realists" show at the Sidney Janis Gallery, New York City.

1963

February	One-man show at the Richard Feigen Gallery, Chicago, and "Gayety," happening at the University of Chicago.
April	"Stars," happening commissioned by the Gallery of Modern Art, Washington, D.C.
August	Gave up 2nd Street Store and moved to Venice, California.
October	One-man show at the Dwan Gallery, Los Angeles.
December	"Autobodys," happening for automobiles in Los Angeles. "Bedroom Ensemble" constructed.

1964

January	"Bedroom Ensemble" shown in "Four Environments," group show (with Dine, Segal and Rosenquist) at Sidney Janis Gallery.
March	Returned to New York. First one-man show at the Sidney Janis Gallery.
April	Traveled to Venice, Italy.
June-September	American Pavilion, Venice Biennale, Italy.
October	Worked in Paris. One-man show at Ileana Sonnabend Gallery, Paris.
November	Worked for two weeks at di Laurentiis Studios, Rome, on a film for Michelangelo Antonioni.
November	Returned to New York. Resided at Chelsea Hotel until March 1965.

1965

March	Rented large new studio on 14th Street, New York City.
May	First showing of "Colossal Monuments" in a group show, "New Work," at Sidney Janis Gallery.
May	"Washes," happening at Al Roon's Health Club, sponsored by the First New York Theater Rally.
June	"Birth of the Flag," filmed version of "Washes" in outdoor site.
August	Began first "multiple" productions—editions of "Baked Potato" and "Tea Bag" objects.
December	"Moviehouse," happening at the Film Makers' Cinematheque, 41st Street Theater, New York City.

1966

April	One-man show at Sidney Janis Gallery—"Airflow" subject and Bathroom Group.
September	One-man show, work of 1963-66, Moderna Museet, Stockholm.
October	"Massage," happening at the Moderna Museet.
October	Worked in London. Began object edition of "London Knees" at Edition Alecto.
November	One-man show at Robert Fraser Gallery, London.
December	Returned to New York City to complete "Store Days"—collected notes and photos from the "Store" period.

1967

January	Group show (with Dine and Segal) at the Ontario Gallery of Art, Toronto, Canada.
April	One-man show, Sidney Janis Gallery—Giant Fan, ghost version, and monuments proposals.
April	Black vinyl version of Giant Fan shown in the American Pavilion, Expo 67, Montreal, Canada.
August	Worked in Aspen, Colorado. Drawings at the Aspen Center of Contemporary Art.
August	"Bedroom Ensemble" shown at the Saõ Paolo Biennale, Brazil. "Drum Set" shown at the Guggenheim Museum, New York City.
October	"Hole" dug in Central Park as part of the "Sculptures in Environment" show sponsored by the New York Parks Commission.
November	Group show of studies for the Frank O'Hara memorial volume *Memory of My Feelings*, Museum of Modern Art, New York City.
November	One-man show of monuments proposals for the opening of the Museum of Contemporary Art, Chicago.
December	Lithographs at Mourlot workshop, New York City.

1968

January	Began work with Gemini G.E.L., printmakers in Los Angeles—"Notes," "Airflow" series, and "Punching Bag Noses," in editions, using lithography and other media.
May	One-man show at the Irving Blum Gallery, Los Angeles.
June	"Dokumenta IV", Kassel, West Germany.
August	Attended Democratic convention in Chicago.
September	"Chicago Fireplug," object in edition, for Richard Feigen Graphics, New York City.
October	Group show protesting violence used by the Democratic convention, Richard Feigen Gallery, Chicago.
October	"Earthworks" at the Dwan Gallery, New York City 1969.
December	"Annual Exhibition: Sculpture," Whitney Museum of American Art, New York City.
December	Prepared "The Typewriter," a happening in script form, commissioned by *Esquire* magazine (published May 1969).
December	Models made for Giant Hard Saw, to be executed in Vancouver, Canada.

1969

January   "New York 13," group show traveling Canada. Visited Vancouver to install Giant Hard Saw.

January   Soft Picasso—soft version of maquette for Chicago Picasso, commissioned by Letter Edged in Black Press for use in a lawsuit over copyright of the sculpture by the city of Chicago.

January-June   Replica of the "Bedroom Ensemble" designed and assembled, including the original gallery site. Visits to Los Angeles.

March-April   "When Attitudes Become Form: Works-Concepts-Processes-Situations-Information," Kunsthalle, Bern.

April   One-man show at Richard Feigen Gallery, Chicago. First models of "feasible" monuments proposals.

May   Group show, "New Work," at Sidney Janis Gallery.

May   Set up new studio in warehouse, New Haven, Connecticut, to work on large-scale outdoor sculpture.

May   First "feasible" monument realized—a 24 ft. high "Giant Lipstick on Caterpillar Base," subscribed by students at the Yale School of Art and Architecture and donated to the University.

May   Began "feasible" monuments projects at Walt Disney workshops, Burbank, California, for the "Art and Technology" project sponsored by the Los Angeles County Museum.

June   Visited London to supervise completion and installation of "Bedroom Ensemble" replica, for "Pop Art" exhibition at the Hayward Gallery.

September   "Claes Oldenburg," exhibition at the Museum of Modern Art, traveling to Amsterdam and London.

Catalogue Raisonné of Drawings, 1958-1967

This catalogue covers the years 1958-1967. It lists the drawings which have passed into collections during that time, by sale or by gift. A selection of drawings from the artist's collection and that of his wife is also included. These drawings were selected by the artist and Gene Baro. A few of the drawings which have left the studio are not yet accounted for.

The drawings here catalogued are signed, with few exceptions, in the lower right corner, usually with the artist's initials (C.O.), followed by the year or its last two numerals. In certain drawings, initials are also contained in the drawing itself.

The titles in this catalogue were given by the artist at the time of compilation, and are meant to be definitive—filling the lack of titles, replacing casual titles or titles given by dealers and collectors in cases where the artist had not earlier supplied a title.

The technique description "crayon and watercolor" covers: litho, wax, conte, and water-soluble crayons; casein, tempera, transparent watercolors; and inks (colored or black) used as wash.

Monoprints are listed as drawings. They are executed in India ink on glass. Multiple editions which are objects rather than drawings are not included.

Provenance is abbreviated as follows: 1. David Anderson Gallery, New York; 2. Dwan Gallery, Los Angeles and New York; 3. Robert Fraser Gallery, London; 4. Green Gallery, New York; 5. Sidney Janis Gallery, New York. Others are listed by name. Where no provenance or collection is listed, the drawings are presently kept for sale by the Sidney Janis Gallery in New York.

In addition to the drawings listed in the Catalogue Raisonné and the uncatalogued drawings (larger and unbound) in the artist's collection, drawing activity has included numerous plans and templates used in executing pieces from the beginning of 1963 to the present. There are also notebooks of small rapid sketches, collected according to periods and place and mounted on sheets of paper 8 ½ × 11 inches, in pressure binders. There are about fifty binders at present. The contents are subject to rearrangement.

C.O.

The Catalogue Raisonné is the result of nearly two years of research. However, a few drawings may not have been included. It would be appreciated if anyone owning a drawing not listed here would write to Paul Bianchini at Chelsea House Publishers, 70 W. 40th Street, New York, providing information on the drawing for possible inclusion in future editions or supplements.

*1 STREET EVENT—WOMAN BEATING CHILD 1958
Pen and watercolor, 7½ × 5 in.
The artist, New York

*2 CIRCUS GIRL ON BIG BALL 1958
Crayon, 6¾ × 5 in.
The artist, New York

3 PAT SITTING ON COT 1959
Crayon, 9¼ × 12⅞ in.
Mr. and Mrs. Tom Wesselmann, New York

4 PAT SEATED IN A CHAIR 1959
Crayon, 13⅞ × 10⅞ in.
Provenance : 4
Collection of Emily B. Staempfli, New York

5 PAT SITTING ON COT IN STRIPED SWEATER 1959
Crayon, 12 × 17½ in.
Provenance : Dayton's Gallery 12, Minneapolis, Minnesota
Mr. and Mrs. Louis Zelle, St. Paul, Minnesota

*6 PAT IN BLACK UNDERWEAR, SEATED 1959
Crayon, 14 × 10¾ in.
Gene Baro, London, England

7 PAT, FROM BACK, IN BLACK UNDERWEAR, STANDING BY EASEL 1959
Crayon, 13¾ × 10¾ in.
Mr. and Mrs. Marcus Ratliff, New York

*8 PAT LYING WITH LEGS APART IN SLIP 1959
Crayon, 10 × 13¾ in.
The artist, New York

*9 PAT, NUDE, IN CHAIR, WITH BLACK BAND AROUND WAIST 1959
Crayon, 8¾ × 11⅞ in.
Mrs. Claes Oldenburg, New York

*10 PAT, BENT FORWARD, SHAKING HER HAIR DOWN 1959
Crayon, 14 × 16⅝ in.
The artist, New York

11 PAT, NUDE, ON STOOL, WITH PROFILE OF CAT 1959
Crayon, 7 × 9½ in.
Mr. and Mrs. Gösta Oldenburg, New York

*12 PAT STANDING, FROM SIDE—"MONKEY WOMAN" 1959
Crayon, 35 × 23½ in.
The artist, New York

*13   PAT, NUDE, SEATED, FROM BEHIND 1959
Crayon, 13⅝×10 in.
The artist, New York

*14   PAT, NUDE, SLEEPING WITH CAT 1959
Crayon, 10×13¾ in.
The artist, New York

*15   PAT SEATED, WITH HAIR OVER HER FACE 1959
Crayon, 11¾×17½ in.
The artist, New York

*16   PAT, WITH PIGTAIL, FROM BEHIND, IN LENOX STUDIO 1959
Crayon, 14×16½ in.
The artist, New York

17   PAT READING IN BED, LENOX 1959
Crayon, 12×17½ in.
Provenance: Dayton's Gallery 12, Minneapolis, Minnesota,
Miss Felice Wender, Minneapolis, Minnesota

18   PAT SITTING ON A HAMMOCK, LENOX 1959
Crayon, 11½×17 in.
Mr. and Mrs. Gösta Oldenburg, New York

*19   HOUSE BETWEEN TREES, CASTING A SHADOW, LENOX 1959
Crayon, 12×17½ in.
Provenance: 5; Dayton's Gallery 12, Minneapolis, Minnesota
Paul Bianchini, New York

20   ENTRANCE TO AN ESTATE, LENOX 1959
Crayon, 11¾×17½ in.
The artist, New York

21   ROUAULT 1959
Monoprint, 19½×25 in.
Raymond Saroff, New York

22   TWO GUYS ON THE STREET WITH TALK BALLOONS 1959
Monoprint, 17¾×11¾ in.
The artist, New York

23   TWO HEADS WITH TALK BALLOONS 1959
Ink, 16½×14 in.
Provenance: 4
Collection of Mr. and Mrs. Robert B. Mayer, Winnetka, Illinois

24   DINE-CLAES POSTER—STUDY FOR A POSTER ANNOUNCING TWO-MAN SHOW
AT JUDSON GALLERY 1959
Ink, 17×12 in.
David Anderson, New York

25   GRAND SPEAKER 1959
Ink, 23½ × 17¾ in.
Harry N. Abrams Family Collection, New York

*26   STREET POEM—MOON POP 1959
Ink, 18 × 16¼ in.
The artist, New York

27   THE STREET 1959
Ink, 16½ × 13¾ in.
Provenance : 4
Washington Gallery of Modern Art, Washington, D.C.

28   RAY GUN 1959
Ink, 16½ × 13¾ in.
Provenance : 4
Collection of Mr. and Mrs. Robert C. Scull, New York

29   RAY GUN PISSER 1959
Ink, 14 × 10 in.
Professor Hanford Yang, New York

*30   DUBUFFET-CELINE-FRENCHMEN 1959
Ink, 16¼ × 11¾ in.
Provenance : 4
Collection of Mr. and Mrs. Robert C. Scull, New York

*31   RAY GUN POSTER—AIRPLANE FACE 1960
Monoprint, 17¾ × 11⅞ in.
The artist, New York

32   RAY GUN POSTER 1960
Monoprint, 22 × 16 in.
David Anderson, New York

33   STREET DRAWING WITH GIRL—RA 1960
Ink, 13⅞ × 10⅞ in.
Mr. and Mrs. Abe Adler, Los Angeles, California

34   BOX BOX RIVERA 1960
Ink, 13½ × 10 in.
Seymour Schweber, Kings Point, New York

35   STREET POEM—ESER ARTSE 1960
Ink, 18 × 23½ in.
David Anderson, New York

*36   PROFILE OF STREET CHICK, CUT FROM MAGAZINE COVER 1960
Cut-out and watercolor, 11⅝ in. high
The artist, New York

50   FIRST VERSION OF ANNOUNCEMENT, REUBEN GALLERY ONE-MAN SHOW *(not used)* 1960
Ink, 10×13½ in.
The artist, New York

*51   ORIGINAL FOR ANNOUNCEMENT, REUBEN GALLERY ONE-MAN SHOW   1960
Ink on newspaper, 13½×10¼ in.
The artist, New York

*52   YA BLA AND MAN IN CAR   1960
Monoprint, 24×18 in.
The artist, New York

*53   TENEMENT, EMPIRE SIGN, AND AIRPLANE   1960
Monoprint, 24×18 in.
The artist, New York

*54   VAN   1960
Cardboard, oil wash, and wood, 12¼×13 in.
Mrs. Claes Oldenburg, New York

*55   CAR ON A FRAGMENT OF STREET   1960
Cardboard, oil wash, and spray enamel, 13½×31½ in.
The artist, New York

*56   STREET FRAGMENT WITH CAR AND GIRL WALKING   1960
Cardboard, paper, and turpentine wash, with movable "leg", 31×22 in.
The artist, New York

57   STREET FIGURE—MAN WITH MANHOLE   1960
Collage and watercolor, 24×18 in.
The artist, New York

*58   EMPIRE SIGN—WITH M AND I DELETED   1960
Cardboard and oil wash, 54½×23¾ in.
The artist, New York

*59   STREET SIGN   1960
Cardboard and oil wash, both sides, 104×41½ in.
The artist, New York

60   POSTER STUDY—"NEW MEDIA, NEW FORMS I," MARTHA JACKSON GALLERY   1960
Collage, ink, and watercolor, 24×18½ in.
Provenance : 4
Collection of Mr. and Mrs. Robert C. Scull, New York

61   POSTER STUDY—"NEW MEDIA, NEW FORMS I," MARTHA JACKSON GALLERY   1960
Collage, ink, and watercolor, 24×18¾ in.
Provenance : 4
Eleanor Riegelhaupt, Boston, Massachusetts

*62 POSTER—"NEW MEDIA, NEW FORMS I," MARTHA JACKSON GALLERY 1960
Photoengraving (original lost), 22 ⅝ × 17 ¾ in.
The artist, New York

63 BIG CARDBOARD FLAG 1960
Ink on cardboard, 22 × 38 in.
David Anderson, New York

*64 FLAG TO FOLD IN THE POCKET 1960
Ink, 29½ × 47 in. (unfolded)
The artist, New York

65 BUTCHER-PAPER FLAG 1960
Ink and silver foil, 9 × 12 in.
Dr. Doris Neuerburg, Cologne, West Germany

66 FLAG ON "CONNECT THE NUMBERS" 1960
Ink on newspaper, 8 × 11 in.
David Anderson, New York

67 MAN AND WOMAN TALKING 1960
Ink, 14 × 11 in.
Mrs. Claes Oldenburg, New York

68 MEN WITH NOSES 1960
Crayon, 14 × 16¾ in.
Carl Lehmann-Haupt, New York

*69 NUDE FIGURE WITH AMERICAN FLAG—A B C HOORAY 1960
Ink and watercolor, 11 × 8½ in.
Mrs. Claes Oldenburg, New York

*70 SKETCH FOR A SCENE IN A PERFORMANCE 1960
Crayon and pencil, 11 × 8½ in.
The artist, New York

71 STUDY USING AN AMERICAN FLAG 1960
Crayon and watercolor, 13½ × 10 in.
The artist, New York

*72 STUDY USING AN AMERICAN FLAG 1960
Chalk and crayon, 13½ × 10 in.
The artist, New York

*73 OBJECTS FROM THE WINDOW OF A LINGERIE SHOP—GIRDLE,
STOCKINGS, BRA 1960
Ink, 8¾ × 6¼ in.
The artist, New York

*74   STREET CHICK FROM THE SIDE, AS IF IN WINDOW, WITH
      FORTY-NINE CENTS SIGN 1960
      Chalk and pencil, 11 × 8½ in.
      The artist, New York

*75   POSTER FOR A PROJECTED PERFORMANCE—INJUN 1960
      Monoprint and watercolor, 16¾ × 13⅞ in.
      The artist, New York

*76   POSTER FOR "BLACKOUTS"—BUTTER AND JAM 1960
      Monoprint, 16¾ × 13⅛ in.
      The artist, New York

77   POSTER FOR "BLACKOUTS"—ERASERS 1960
      Monoprint, 17¾ × 14 in.
      The artist, New York

*78   SKETCH FOR A DANCE COSTUME—BLUE DISCS, BIG RED HAT 1961
      Pencil and watercolor, 10 × 7½ in.
      The artist, New York

79   SKETCH FOR A DANCE COSTUME 1961
      Pencil and watercolor, 10 × 7⅞ in.
      Edith Adams, New York

80   AMERICAN FLAG 1961
      Crayon and watercolor, 13½ × 10 in.
      Jack Glenn, Kansas City, Missouri

81   STORE SKETCH—REBEL 1961
      Ink and watercolor, 12 × 17½ in.
      David Anderson, New York

82   STORE SKETCH—24 HOURS 1961
      Ink and watercolor, 12 × 17½ in.
      Herbert Barrows, Ann Arbor, Michigan

83   USA AND FLAG ON STAFF, WITH NAMES CAESAR ROMEO CARMEN 1961
      Ink, 11⅞ × 17⅝ in.
      Mr. and Mrs. William Ash, Brooklyn, New York

84   MAN AND WOMAN PROFILES, SHIRT, CARMEN 1961
      Ink, 11⅞ × 17⅝ in.
      Mr. and Mrs. William Ash, Brooklyn, New York

85   HAT, GIRDLE ON SIDE, CARMEN REBEL 1961
      Ink, 11⅞ × 17⅝ in.
      Mr. and Mrs. William Ash, Brooklyn, New York

86   SHIRT, HAT, PETTICOAT, HEART, TORSO WITH BRA AND GARTERBELT 1961
      Ink, 11⅞ × 17⅝ in.
      Mr. and Mrs. William Ash, Brooklyn, New York

87   STORE WINDOW—HEART, DRESS, DONUT, 39   1961
Crayon and watercolor, 17½×11⅞ in.
The artist, New York

*88   NOTEBOOK SKETCH—FRAGMENT OF A BATHROOM WALL, WITH BATHTUB   1961
Crayon on steno-paper, mounted on sheet, 11×8½ in.
The artist, New York

*89   NOTEBOOK SKETCH—STOCKINGS DISPLAY   1961
Pencil and watercolor, 11×8½ in.
The artist, New York

*90   NOTEBOOK SKETCH—GYM SHOES   1961
Ink, 4¾×3 in.
The artist, New York

*91   THINGS IN A WINDOW—OVOIDS AND A CUBE   1961
Crayon, 12⅛×10½ in.
The artist, New York

92   ANNOUNCEMENT, GREEN GALLERY GROUP SHOW—OBJECTS ON A TABLE TOP, WITH SCRIBBLING   1961
Offset (original lost), 15×9½ in.
The artist, New York

93   INTERIOR OF "THE STORE"—SKETCH FOR A POSTER *(not executed)*   1961
Crayon and watercolor, 23½×18 in.
Mr. and Mrs. Richard E. Oldenburg, New York

94   ROUGH FOR A POSTER ADVERTISING "THE STORE"   1961
Cut-out paper and watercolor on printed poster, 22×27¾ in.
The artist, New York

95   TUXEDO JACKET   1961
Enamel and plaster on newspaper, 20½×25½ in.
Raymond Saroff, New York

96   STUDIES FOR STORE OBJECTS—STOCKING LEGS, FROZEN CUSTARD   1961
Collage, crayon, and watercolor, 18⅝×23⅞ in.
Collection of Mr. and Mrs. Robert C. Scull, New York
Note: Mounted in 1963 and signed "1963" at that time. The parts of the collage were done in 1961.

97   STUDIES FOR STORE OBJECTS—A SOCK AND FIFTEEN CENTS   1961
Collage, crayon, and watercolor, 23⅞×18⅝ in.
Collection of Mr. and Mrs. Robert C. Scull, New York
Note: Mounted in 1962 and signed "C O 6 2" at that time. The parts of the collage were done in 1961.

98   STUDIES FOR STORE OBJECTS—WATCH, PIE, FROZEN CUSTARD, FIFTEEN CENTS   1961
Collage, crayon, and watercolor, 14⅜×20 in.
Collection of Mr. and Mrs. Robert C. Scull, New York

*99　STUDIES FOR STORE OBJECTS—PIE, 7-UP, FLAG, ORANGES, FIFTEEN CENTS　1961
Collage, crayon, and watercolor, 15×20 in.
Mr. and Mrs. Burton G. Tremaine, New York

100　STUDIES FOR STORE OBJECTS—PETTICOAT, FLAG, GUN　1961
Collage, crayon, and watercolor, 17×13 in.
Provenance: Aaron Siskind, New York
Mr. and Mrs. George Sturman, Chicago, Illinois

101　SILVER TORSO WITH BROWN UNDERWEAR　1961
Enamel on newspaper, 22×16 in.
Professor Hanford Yang, New York

102　BROWN STOCKING LEG AGAINST SILVER　1961
Enamel on newspaper, 22×15 in.
Professor Hanford Yang, New York

103　STORE POSTER—TORN OUT LETTERS, NEWSPAPER PIE, CUPCAKES,
AND HOT DOG　1961
Crayon, enamel, and watercolor, 20×26 in.
Professor Hanford Yang, New York

104　STORE WINDOW—MAN'S SHIRT, MANNEKIN TORSO, 39—ON FRAGMENT　1961
Crayon and watercolor, 18×21 in. (irregular outline)
Professor Hanford Yang, New York

105　STORE WINDOW—SHIRT, HOT DOG　1961
Crayon and watercolor, 12×17½ in.
Professor Hanford Yang, New York

106　NEEDLE AND THREAD, RAZORBLADE, BOTTLECAP, PIECE OF CAKE　1961
Monoprint and watercolor, 18×20 in.
The artist, New York

107　PIE SLICE WITH RECTANGLE　1961
Monoprint and watercolor, 18×24 in.
The artist, New York

*108　CAP　1961
Monoprint and watercolor, 24×18 in.
The artist, New York

*109　RAY GUN POSTER　1961
Sprayed oil wash on torn paper, 24×18 in.
The artist, New York

110　POSTER ANNOUNCING A PERFORMANCE—VOYAGES　1961
Monoprint and watercolor, 17½×23½ in.
Mr. and Mrs. Richard E. Oldenburg, New York

*111   STORE POSTER   1961
Dripped and pressed enamel, 12 × 17½ in.
The artist, New York

112   STUDY FOR ANNOUNCEMENT OF DANCE CONCERT BY AILEEN PASSLOFF DANCE
COMPANY—DANCING FIGURE   1961
Dripped enamel, 12 × 17½ in.
Harry N. Abrams Family Collection, New York

*113   STUDY FOR ANNOUNCEMENT OF DANCE CONCERT BY AILEEN PASSLOFF DANCE
COMPANY—DANCING FIGURE   1962
Dripped enamel, 17½ × 12 in.
The artist, New York

114   STUDY FOR ANNOUNCEMENT OF DANCE CONCERT BY AILEEN PASSLOFF
DANCE COMPANY   1962
Dripped enamel, 17½ × 12 in.
The artist, New York

115   ORIGINAL FOR ANNOUNCEMENT OF DANCE CONCERT BY AILEEN PASSLOFF
DANCE COMPANY—FIGURE STRIDING OVER LANDSCAPE   1962
Dripped enamel, 12 × 17½ in.
Mr. and Mrs. Richard E. Oldenburg, New York

116   STUDIES FOR STORE OBJECTS—TOY SAILBOATS, CUPCAKE, AND ICE CREAM
CONE   1962
Collage, crayon, and watercolor, 11¾ × 17¾ in.
Mr. and Mrs. Jim Dine, New York

*117   STORE OBJECTS—WATCH IN CASE, CUPCAKES, SOCK   1962
Ink and watercolor, 6 × 8¾ in.
The artist, New York

118   STUDY FOR A SOFT SCULPTURE IN THE FORM OF A SAILBOAT   1962
Crayon and watercolor, 10 × 13½ in.
Harry N. Abrams Family Collection, New York

119   STUDY FOR SOFT SCULPTURES IN THE FORMS OF A PLANE, A SAILBOAT,
AND A CONE   1962
Crayon and watercolor, 10 × 13½ in.
Harry N. Abrams Family Collection, New York

120   LEGS   1962
Crayon and watercolor, 10 × 13½ in.
Harry N. Abrams Family Collection, New York

121   SEX ACT   1962
Crayon and watercolor, 8¾ × 10¾ in.
Mr. and Mrs. Alfred Ordover, New York

122 SANDWICH 1962
Crayon and watercolor, 11 × 13½ in.
Joan Kron, Philadelphia, Pennsylvania

123 CAKE SLICE 1962
Watercolor, 9¹⁵/₁₆ × 13½ in.

124 HAMBURGER 1962
Crayon and watercolor, 10 × 13¼ in.
Mrs. Solomon Kushner, Fontana Gallery, Narberth, Pennsylvania

*125 NOTEBOOK SKETCH—FIFTY-SEVENTH STREET 1962
Crayon, 11 × 8½ in.
The artist, New York

*126 SKETCH TOWARD A SOFT SCULPTURE IN THE FORM OF A GIANT MAN 1962
Crayon and watercolor, 11 × 13¾ in.
The artist, New York

127 SKETCH FOR A SOFT SCULPTURE IN THE FORM OF A CAKE WEDGE—WOMAN
FOR SCALE 1962
Crayon and watercolor, 14 × 11½ in.
Dayton's Gallery 12, Minneapolis, Minnesota

*128 GIANT SOFT SCULPTURES VISUALIZED IN GREEN GALLERY—HAT AND SHIRT 1962
Crayon and watercolor, 11½ × 17½ in.
The artist, New York

129 GIANT SOFT SCULPTURES VISUALIZED IN GREEN GALLERY—CONE,
SANDWICH, HAT 1962
Crayon and watercolor, 10 × 13½ in.
The artist, New York

*130 ORIGINAL FOR POSTER ANNOUNCING ONE-MAN SHOW AT GREEN GALLERY—
BIPLANE 1962
Crayon, 13⅞ × 16⅞ in.
Provenance : 4
Jonathan D. Scull, New York

131 FREIGHTER 1962
Crayon, 26½ × 39⅞ in.
Provenance : Richard Feigen Gallery, Chicago, Illinois
William Harris, New York

*132 CAKE WEDGE 1962
Crayon, 25 × 32⅜ in.
Provenance : 4
Collection of Mr. and Mrs. Robert C. Scull, New York

133 ICE CREAM CONE 1962
Crayon, 13¼ × 16¼ in.
Provenance : 4
Lewis Pollock, Lexington, Massachusetts

134 HAMBURGER 1962
Crayon, 14 × 17 in.
Provenance : 4
Museum of Modern Art, New York

135 SOFT LETTERS AND NUMBERS 1963
Ink, 8 × 5⅜ in.
Allen Art Museum, Oberlin, Ohio

136 MAP OF CHICAGO STUFFED WITH SOFT NUMBERS 1963
Ink, 12 × 9½ in.
Harry Bouras, Chicago, Illinois

137 MAP OF CHICAGO STUFFED WITH SOFT NUMBERS 1963
Crayon, 23¾ × 18 in.
Provenance : 5
Byron Gallery, New York

138 SOFT NUMBERS IN IRREGULAR AREA 1963
Ink, 12 × 9½ in.
Dwan Gallery, New York

139 WEDDING CAKE 1963
Crayon, watercolor, and ink, 13½ × 10¾ in.
Provenance : 5 ; Dayton's Gallery 12, Minneapolis, Minnesota
Mrs. Herbert Fischbach, New York

140 DOLL HOUSE 1963
Crayon and watercolor, 13½ × 10¾ in.
Provenance : 5
Franklin Siden, Detroit, Michigan

*141 NOTEBOOK SKETCH—SILK SUMMER SHIRT 1963
Crayon, pencil, and watercolor, 7⅞ × 5⅜ in., mounted on sheet 11 × 8½ in.
The artist, New York

*142 NOTEBOOK SKETCH—MATERIAL AND SCISSORS 1963
Ink and watercolor, 11 × 8½ in.
The artist, New York

*143 NOTEBOOK SKETCH—POOL TABLE 1963
Ink, 11 × 8½ in.
The artist, New York

144 NEW YORK DRESSES 1963
Crayon and watercolor, 18½ × 24 in.
Provenance : 2
William Rockhill Nelson Gallery of Art, Kansas City, Missouri

145 TWO SUITS 1963
Crayon and watercolor, 18¾ × 23¾ in.
Mr. and Mrs. George Sturman, Chicago, Illinois

146 BIPLANE 1963
Ink, 8½ × 11 in.
John Weber, New York

147 WOMAN'S LEGS ATTACHED TO A CHAIR 1963
Crayon and watercolor, 23½ × 18 in.
Mr. and Mrs. Sidney Lehrer, New York

148 BAKED POTATO 1963
Crayon and watercolor, 14⅝ × 12⅛ in.
John Weber, New York

149 ICE CREAM SUNDAE 1963
Crayon and watercolor, 14¾ × 11 in.
Mr. and Mrs. Leonard Brown, Springfield, Massachusetts

150 HOT DOGS AROUND A CUP OF MUSTARD WITH A SPOON 1963
Crayon and watercolor, 18 × 23½ in.
Mr. and Mrs. Richard M. Polsky, New York

151 BAG OF POTATO CHIPS 1963
Crayon and watercolor, 13¾ × 11 in.
The artist, New York

*152 CIGARETTE WITH SOLID SMOKE AND SHAVING BRUSH 1963
Crayon and watercolor, 11 × 14 in.
The artist, New York

*153 STUDY FOR SOFT TYPEWRITER 1963
Crayon and watercolor, 11½ × 13⅝ in.
Mr. and Mrs. Peter J. Solomon, New York

154 SKETCH OF A TYPEWRITER 1963
Pencil and watercolor, 11 × 13¾ in.
Mr. and Mrs. Erik Lindegren, Stockholm, Sweden

155 STUDY FOR A SOFT SCULPTURE IN THE FORM OF A PAY TELEPHONE 1963
Watercolor on newspaper, 42 × 28 in.
Provenance: 2
Dr. and Mrs. Nathan Alpers, Los Angeles, California

156 DRESSING TABLE 1963
Crayon and watercolor, 13½ × 10¾ in.
Provenance: 5
Collection of John and Kimiko Powers, Aspen, Colorado

157 REFRIGERATOR 1963
Crayon, pencil, and watercolor, 13¾ × 11 in.
Provenance: 5; Leon Kraushar, New York; Karl Ströher, Darmstadt, West Germany
Private collection, New York

158　HOME INTERIOR WITH STUFFED CHAIR AND TV　1963
Crayon and watercolor, 16¾×14 in.
Provenance : 5 ; Leon Kraushar, New York
Collection Karl Ströher, Darmstadt, West Germany

159　CHAIR　1963
Crayon and watercolor, 13½×10¾ in.
Provenance : 5 ; Leon Kraushar, New York ; Karl Ströher, Darmstadt, West Germany
Private collection, New York

160　ZEBRA CHAIR　1963
Crayon and watercolor, 24×15 in.
Provenance : 5
Dr. John A. Cook, New York

161　IRONING BOARD　1963
Chalk, crayon, and watercolor, 23½×18 in.
Provenance : Jon Nicolas Streep
Mr. and Mrs. M. Hirsch, Los Angeles, California

162　STUDY FOR ANNOUNCEMENT FOR ONE-MAN SHOW AT DWAN GALLERY—
MICKEY MOUSE　1963
Crayon, 16¾×14 in.
Provenance : 5
Gordon Locksley Gallery, Minneapolis, Minnesota

163　STUDY FOR ANNOUNCEMENT FOR ONE-MAN SHOW AT DWAN GALLERY—
MICKEY MOUSE　1963
Crayon and watercolor, 24×18 in.
Provenance : 5
Collection of John and Kimiko Powers, Aspen, Colorado

*164　STUDY FOR ANNOUNCEMENT FOR ONE-MAN SHOW AT DWAN GALLERY—
MICKEY MOUSE WITH RED HEART　1963
Crayon and watercolor, 17×14 in.
Provenance : 5
Private collection, New York

165　STUDY FOR ANNOUNCEMENT FOR ONE-MAN SHOW AT DWAN GALLERY—
ICE CREAM CONE UPSIDE DOWN WITH MICKEY MOUSE HEAD　1963
Crayon and watercolor, 14×16¾ in.
Provenance : 5
Mr. and Mrs. Horace H. Solomon, New York

166　STUDY FOR ANNOUNCEMENT FOR ONE-MAN SHOW AT DWAN GALLERY—
ICE CREAM CONE UPSIDE DOWN WITH SMALL MICKEY MOUSE HEAD　1963
Crayon and watercolor, 24×18 in.
Provenance : 5
Carroll Janis, New York

167 STUDY FOR ANNOUNCEMENT FOR ONE-MAN SHOW AT DWAN GALLERY—
GOOD HUMOR ICE CREAM BAR 1963
Crayon and watercolor, 24×18 in.

*168 STUDY FOR ANNOUNCEMENT FOR ONE-MAN SHOW AT DWAN GALLERY—
GOOD HUMOR ICE CREAM BAR 1963
Crayon and watercolor, 17×14 in.
The artist, New York

169 STUDY FOR ANNOUNCEMENT FOR ONE-MAN SHOW AT DWAN GALLERY—
GOOD HUMOR ICE CREAM BAR 1963
Crayon and watercolor, 30×22 in.
Provenance : 5
Öster Fagerlin, Mo och Domsjö, Sweden

*170 VISUALIZATION OF A GIANT SOFT SCULPTURE IN THE FORM OF A SHIRT
WITH TIE 1963
Crayon and watercolor, 14×16½ in.
Provenance : 2
Collection of Mr. and Mrs. Michael Blankfort, Los Angeles, California

*171 GIANT KITCHEN CHAIR ON ITS SIDE—CHROME-HOME 1963
Crayon and watercolor, 13 ⅞×16 ⅝ in.
The artist, New York

172 SKETCH OF A TOILET FROM OVERHEAD 1963
Crayon and watercolor, 16 ¾× 14 in.
Provenance : 5; Leon Kraushar, New York
Collection of Karl Ströher, Darmstadt, West Germany

173 TWO PURSES FROM A LOS ANGELES BILLBOARD 1963
Crayon and watercolor, 14×17 in.
Provenance : 5
Emily Rauh, St. Louis, Missouri

174 STUDY FOR A POSTER FOR "4 ENVIRONMENTS," SIDNEY JANIS GALLERY—
THE HOME 1963
Crayon and watercolor, 24×18 in.
Provenance: 5
Collection of John and Kimiko Powers, Aspen, Colorado

*175 STUDY FOR A POSTER FOR "4 ENVIRONMENTS," SIDNEY JANIS GALLERY—
THE HOME 1963
Crayon and watercolor, 24×18 in.
Provenance : 5 ; Paul Bianchini, New York
The Joan and Lester Avnet Collection, New York

*176 STUDY OF BED WITH BEDTABLES—BEDROOM ENSEMBLE 1963
Chalk and spray enamel, 26½×41 in.
Provenance : 3
Dr. Hubert Peeters Van Hoorenbeeck, Bruges, Belgium

177   STUDY FOR PILLOWS—BEDROOM ENSEMBLE   1963
      Crayon and ink, 18×24 in.
      Provenance : 5
      Christopher Gibbs, London, England

178   STUDY FOR BED AND DRESSER—BEDROOM ENSEMBLE   1963
      Crayon and watercolor, 18×23¾ in.
      Provenance : 5 ; Paul Bianchini, New York
      Mr. and Mrs. Robert Bernhard, Port Chester, New York

179   STUDY FOR ZEBRA CHAIR—BEDROOM ENSEMBLE   1963
      Chalk and watercolor, 26½×41 in.
      Provenance : 5
      Collection of John and Kimiko Powers, Aspen, Colorado

180   STUDY FOR TABLE OBJECTS—BEDROOM ENSEMBLE   1963
      Crayon and watercolor, 14½×17 in.
      Provenance : 5 ; Gordon Locksley Gallery, Minneapolis, Minnesota
      Mr. and Mrs. Jan vander Marck, Chicago, Illinois

181   STUDY FOR BEDTABLE AND LAMP—BEDROOM ENSEMBLE   1963
      Crayon and pencil, 14×16¾ in.
      The artist, New York

182   STUDY FOR A POSTER FOR ONE-MAN SHOW AT SIDNEY JANIS GALLERY—
      TABLE LAMP ON DRESSER *(not executed)*   1963
      Crayon and watercolor, 23¾×18 in.

183   STUDY OF AN ELECTRIC SAW   1964
      Chalk, spray enamel, and watercolor, 40×26 in.

184   NOTEBOOK SKETCH—ALTERED NEWSPAPER CLIPPING OF A PING-PONG
      TABLE   1964
      Watercolor on newspaper clipping, 11×8½ in.
      Moderna Museet, Stockholm, Sweden

*185 STUDY FOR A SCULPTURE IN THE FORM OF A PING-PONG TABLE   1964
      Chalk, collage, and watercolor, 26½×41 in.
      Provenance : 5 ; Collection Buckwalter, Kansas City, Missouri ; Paul Bianchini, New York ;
      Dwan Gallery, New York
      Dr. and Mrs. Judd Marmor, Los Angeles, California

186   STUDY FOR A SCULPTURE COMBINING A PING-PONG TABLE
      AND A POOL TABLE   1964
      Ink and watercolor, 18×23 in.

187   STUDY FOR A PING-PONG PADDLE   1964
      Ink and watercolor, 18×23 in.

*188 PLAN FOR A SCULPTURE IN THE FORM OF WALL SWITCHES   1964
      Ink and watercolor, 28⅝×23⅜ in.
      Provenance : 5
      Whitney Museum of American Art, New York, Neysa McMein Purchase Award

189 STUDY FOR A SCULPTURE IN THE FORM OF AN OUTLET AND PLUG 1964
Ink and watercolor, 29×23½ in.
Provenance : 3
Dr. Hubert Peeters Van Hoorenbeeck, Bruges, Belgium

190 STUDY FOR A SCULPTURE IN THE FORM OF AN OUTLET AND PLUG 1964
Pencil and watercolor, 17¾×22¼ in.
Provenance : 5
Gary Smith, New York

191 STUDY FOR A SCULPTURE IN THE FORM OF A VACUUM CLEANER 1964
Ink and watercolor, 23×18 in.
Provenance: 5
William Copley, New York

*192 STUDY FOR A SCULPTURE IN THE FORM OF A VACUUM CLEANER—FROM SIDE 1964
Chalk and watercolor, 40×26 in.
Provenance : 3
Dr. Hubert Peeters Van Hoorenbeeck, Bruges, Belgium

193 A TOILET 1964
Crayon and watercolor, 17¾×23¼ in.
Provenance : 5
Collection of John and Kimiko Powers, Aspen, Colorado

*194 STUDY FOR A SOFT SCULPTURE IN THE FORM OF A TOASTER 1964
Crayon and watercolor, 11½×13½ in.
Provenance : 5 , Leon Kraushar, New York ; Karl Ströher, Darmstadt, West Germany
Private collection, New York

195 THE HAT 1964
Crayon and watercolor, 11½×14 in.
Provenance : 5
Private collection, New York

196 "NUTELLA"—FROM AN ITALIAN BILLBOARD 1964
Crayon and watercolor, 12½×17⅝ in.

197 ESPRESSO CUP ON PLATE 1964
Crayon and watercolor, 12¼×17½ in.
Mr. and Mrs. Sidney Lehrer, New York

198 PARISIAN BANANA SPLIT 1964
Crayon and watercolor, 12¼×17⅝ in.
Provenance : 5
Allen Art Museum, Oberlin, Ohio

199 PARISIAN BANANA SPLIT 1964
Crayon and watercolor, 12¼×17½ in.
Provenance : 5
Private collection, New Haven, Connecticut

200   OUTBOARD MOTOR   1964
Crayon and watercolor, 17½×12¼ in.
Provenance: 5
Collection of Fay Gold, Atlanta, Georgia

201   OUTBOARD MOTOR   1964
Crayon and watercolor, 17½×12¼ in.
Provenance: 5
Adolph O. Susholtz, Houston, Texas

202   CHANTILLY DESSERT   1964
Crayon and watercolor, 12⅜×17⅝ in.

203   CHANTILLY DESSERT—AFTER EATING   1964
Crayon and watercolor, 12¼×17 in.

204   DESIGN FOR A DRESSING TABLE   1964
Crayon and watercolor, 11¾×15½ in.
Mrs. Claes Oldenburg, New York

205   STUDY FOR A SOFT SCULPTURE IN THE FORM OF A BURROUGHS ADDING
      MACHINE   1964
Crayon and watercolor, 17¾×23¾ in.
Provenance: 5
Mr. and Mrs. Richard L. Selle, Chicago, Illinois

*206   PROPOSED COLOSSAL MONUMENT FOR THE BATTERY, N.Y.C.—VACUUM CLEANER,
      VIEW FROM THE UPPER BAY   1965
Crayon and watercolor, 23×29 in.
Provenance: 5
Jonathan D. Scull, New York

207   PROPOSED COLOSSAL MONUMENT FOR THE BATTERY, N.Y.C.—VACUUM CLEANER,
      EAST RIVER VIEW   1965
Crayon and watercolor, 12×17¾ in.
Provenance: 5
Mrs. Robert M. Benjamin, New York

208   PROPOSED COLOSSAL MONUMENT FOR THE BATTERY, N.Y.C.—VACUUM CLEANER,
      VIEW FROM UPPER BAY   1965
Crayon and watercolor, 23×29 in.
Provenance: 5
Jerry Spiegel, New York

*209   PROPOSED COLOSSAL MONUMENT FOR GRAND ARMY PLAZA, N.Y.C.—
      BAKED POTATO   1965
Crayon and watercolor, 18×21¼ in.
Provenance: 5
Collection of Mr. and Mrs. Ira Licht, New York

254

210 PROPOSED COLOSSAL MONUMENT FOR GRAND ARMY PLAZA, N.Y.C.—
BAKED POTATO, THROWN VERSION 1965
Crayon and watercolor, 23 × 29 in.
Provenance : 5
Thomas E. Benesch Memorial Collection, Baltimore Museum of Art, Baltimore, Maryland

211 PROPOSED COLOSSAL MONUMENT FOR GRAND ARMY PLAZA, N.Y.C.—
BAKED POTATO, VIEW FROM ABOVE 1965
Crayon and watercolor, 12 × 17¾ in.
The artist, New York

212 PROPOSED COLOSSAL MONUMENT FOR NEW YORK HARBOR—PIZZA FOR
UPPER BAY 1965
Crayon and watercolor, 12 × 18 in.
Provenance : 5
Mr. and Mrs. Richard L. Selle, Chicago, Illinois

213 PROPOSED COLOSSAL MONUMENT FOR NEW YORK HARBOR—PIZZA FOR
UPPER BAY 1965
Crayon and watercolor, 11¾ × 17½ in.
Provenance : 5
Mr. and Mrs. Edwin Bergman, Chicago, Illinois

214 PROPOSED COLOSSAL MONUMENT FOR NEW YORK HARBOR—PIZZA FOR
UPPER BAY (SCATTERED SLICES) 1965
Crayon and watercolor, 22¾ × 28¾ in.
Provenance : 5
William Wixom, Cleveland, Ohio

215 PROPOSED MONUMENT FOR THE INTERSECTION OF CANAL STREET AND
BROADWAY, N.Y.C.—BLOCK OF CONCRETE, INSCRIBED WITH THE NAMES OF
WAR HEROES 1965
Crayon and watercolor, 11¾ × 17½ in.
Provenance : 5
Mr. and Mrs. Dan Flavin, Cold Spring, New York

*216 PROPOSED COLOSSAL MONUMENT FOR LOWER EAST SIDE—IRONING BOARD 1965
Crayon and watercolor, 21¾ × 29½ in.
Provenance : 5
Mr. and Mrs. Marvin Goodman, Toronto, Canada

217 PROPOSED COLOSSAL MONUMENT FOR LOWER EAST SIDE—IRONING BOARD 1965
Crayon and watercolor, 12 × 17¾ in.
Provenance : 5
Louise Ferrari, Houston, Texas

218 PROPOSED COLOSSAL MONUMENT FOR PARK AVENUE, N.Y.C.—GOOD HUMOR
BAR 1965
Crayon and watercolor, 12 × 17½ in.
Provenance : 5
Mr. and Mrs. Dirk Lohan, Chicago, Illinois

219 PROPOSED COLOSSAL MONUMENT FOR TIMES SQUARE, N.Y.C.—BANANA 1965
Crayon and watercolor, 11½×17¼ in.
Provenance : 5
Mr. and Mrs. Richard L. Selle, Chicago, Illinois

220 PROPOSED COLOSSAL MONUMENT FOR COLUMBUS CIRCLE, N.Y.C.—SILEX
JUICIT 1965
Crayon and watercolor, 29½×21½ in.
Provenance : 5
Mr. and Mrs. Norman B. Champ Jr., St. Louis, Missouri

221 PROPOSED COLOSSAL MONUMENT FOR PATERSON, NEW JERSEY—
CAKE COVER 1965
Crayon and watercolor, 18×23½ in.
Provenance : 5
Mr. and Mrs. Jack Chasnoff, St. Louis, Missouri

222 PROPOSED COLOSSAL MONUMENT FOR CENTRAL PARK NORTH, N.Y.C.—
TEDDY BEAR 1965
Crayon and watercolor, 23×29 in.
Provenance : 5
Alfred Heller, Grass Valley, California

223 PROPOSED COLOSSAL MONUMENT FOR CENTRAL PARK NORTH, N.Y.C.—
TEDDY BEAR 1965
Crayon, 23×30 in.
Provenance : 5
William A.M. Burden, New York

224 PROPOSED COLOSSAL MONUMENT FOR CENTRAL PARK NORTH, N.Y.C.—
TEDDY BEAR 1965
Crayon, 24×19 in.
Mr. and Mrs. Carl E. Cassel, Essex Fells, New Jersey

225 PROPOSED COLOSSAL MONUMENT FOR NEW YORK PARK—TEDDY BEAR
(thrown version) 1965
Crayon and watercolor, 23×29 in.
Provenance : 5
Alfred Heller, Grass Valley, California

226 PROPOSED COLOSSAL MONUMENT FOR TIMES SQUARE, N.Y.C.—BANANA 1965
Crayon and watercolor, 12×17½ in.
Provenance : 5
Mr. and Mrs. William Berman Jr., St. Louis, Missouri

227 PROPOSED COLOSSAL MONUMENT FOR STATEN ISLAND, N.Y.C.—FAN
(study for cover of Domus*)* 1965
Crayon and watercolor, 23½×19 in.
Mr. and Mrs. Richard E. Oldenburg, New York

228 PROPOSED COLOSSAL MONUMENT FOR STATEN ISLAND, N.Y.C.—FAN
(*study for cover of* Domus) 1965
Crayon and watercolor, 19×11½ in.
Provenance : 5
Private collection, Houston, Texas

229 PROPOSED COLOSSAL MONUMENT FOR STATEN ISLAND, N.Y.C.—FAN
(*study for cover of* Domus) 1965
Crayon and watercolor, 14½×11½ in.
Provenance : 5
Mrs. S. Berland, Lawrence, Long Island, New York

230 PROPOSED COLOSSAL MONUMENT FOR ELLIS ISLAND—FRANKFURTER WITH
TOMATO AND TOOTHPICK 1965
Crayon and watercolor, 19⅛×24 in.
Provenance : 5
Collection of Mr. and Mrs. Michael Blankfort, Los Angeles, California

231 PROPOSED COLOSSAL MONUMENT FOR ELLIS ISLAND—SHRIMP 1965
Crayon and watercolor, 12×15½ in.
Provenance : 5
Mr. and Mrs. Dirk Lohan, Chicago, Illinois

*232 PROPOSED MONUMENT FOR THE INTERSECTION OF CANAL STREET AND
BROADWAY, N.Y.C.—BLOCK OF CONCRETE INSCRIBED WITH THE NAMES
OF WAR HEROES 1965
Crayon and watercolor, 15⅞×12 in.
Provenance : 5
Collection of Alicia Legg, New York

233 PROPOSED COLOSSAL MONUMENT FOR CENTRAL PARK NORTH, N.Y.C.—
TEDDY BEAR 1965
Crayon and watercolor, 23×19 in.
Mr. and Mrs. Richard E. Oldenburg, New York

234 PROPOSED COLOSSAL MONUMENT FOR TIMES SQUARE, N.Y.C.—BANANA 1965
Crayon and watercolor, 24½×19 in.
Robert Fraser, London, England

235 PROPOSED COLOSSAL MONUMENT FOR TIMES SQUARE, N.Y.C.—BANANA 1965
Crayon and watercolor, 24½×19 in.
Provenance : 5
Private collection, California

*236 PROPOSED COLOSSAL MONUMENT FOR PARK AVENUE, N.Y.C.—
GOOD HUMOR BAR 1965
Crayon and watercolor, 23½×17½ in.
Provenance : 5
Carroll Janis, New York

237   PROPOSED COLOSSAL MONUMENT FOR PARK AVENUE, N.Y.C.—
GOOD HUMOR BAR 1965
Crayon and watercolor, 16¾ × 13½ in.
Provenance : 5
Collection of Mr. and Mrs. Michael Blankfort, Los Angeles, California

*238   STUDY FOR A SCREENPRINT IN THE FORM OF A PIZZA—PIZZA COMPONENTS
(not executed)
Crayon and watercolor, 16⅝ × 14 in.
The artist, New York

239   STUDY FOR A SCREENPRINT TO ADVERTISE *The Paris Review*—CORNER OF
A MATTRESS 1965
Pencil and spray enamel, 35 × 26 in.
Provenance : 3
Colin Self, Norwich, England

240   STUDY OF FAN BLADES 1965
Crayon and pencil, 41 × 39 in.
Provenance : 5
Collection of John and Kimiko Powers, Aspen, Colorado

241   SKETCH VISUALIZING A SOFT FAN 1965
Crayon and watercolor, 16½ × 13 in.
Provenance : 5
Mrs. Josiah Marvel, Villanova, Pennsylvania

242   SOFT FANS 1965
Crayon and watercolor, 17¾ × 11⅝ in.
Provenance : 5
Mr. and Mrs. Joseph A. Helman, St. Louis, Missouri

243   SOFT NEW YORK 1965
Crayon and watercolor, 16¾ × 13⅝ in.
The artist, New York

244   SKETCH VISUALIZING A SOFT SINK—PINK 1965
Crayon and watercolor, 17½ × 12 in.
Provenance : 5
Dayton's Gallery 12, Minneapolis, Minnesota

245   SKETCH VISUALIZING A SOFT SINK—BLUE 1965
Crayon and watercolor, 23¾ × 18 in.
Provenance : 5
Private collection, New York

246   POACHED EGG 1965
Crayon and watercolor, 13¾ × 16¼ in
Provenance : 5
Mrs. Per Arneberg, New York

247 JUICER 1965
Crayon and watercolor, 13¾ × 16½ in.
Provenance : 5 ; Leon Kraushar, New York
Collection Karl Ströher, Darmstadt, West Germany

248 KETCHUP, THICK AND THIN—FROM A N.Y.C. BILLBOARD 1965
Crayon and watercolor, 17¾ × 12 in.
Provenance : 5
Mrs. Per Arneberg, New York

249 BAKED POTATO, WITH FORK 1965
Crayon and watercolor, 13¾ × 16½ in.
Provenance : 5
Mr. and Mrs. Seymour Propp, New York

250 BAKED POTATO, THROWN IN CORNER, UNDER LIGHT BULB 1965
Crayon and watercolor, 18 × 12 in.
Provenance : 5
Collection of John and Kimiko Powers, Aspen, Colorado

*251 SKETCH OF A 3-WAY PLUG 1965
Crayon and oil wash, 30½ × 23 in.
Provenance : 5
Sam J. Wagstaff, Jr., Detroit, Michigan

252 WOMAN WITH A GIANT PENIS, LEANING ON A STATION WAGON 1965
Pen, 14 × 16¾ in.
Jack Klein, New York

253 CLINICAL STUDY, TOWARDS A HEROIC-EROTIC MONUMENT IN THE ACADEMIC/
COMICS STYLE 1965
Ballpoint pen, 26 × 40 in.
The artist, New York

254 STONE FRANKFURTER WITH CHEESE AND TOMATO 1965
Pencil, 13¾ × 16½ in.

255 STUDY OF A SILEX JUICIT 1965
Crayon, pencil, and watercolor, 30 × 22 in.
Provenance : 5
Collection of John and Kimiko Powers, Aspen, Colorado

*256 BLUE TOILET 1965
Collage, crayon and watercolor, 29¾ × 21¾ in.
Provenance : 3
Dr. Hubert Peeters Van Hoorenbeeck, Bruges, Belgium

*257 STUDY OF A DORMEYER MIXER 1965
Pencil, 30 × 22³⁄₁₆ in.
Provenance : 5
Emily S. Rauh, St. Louis, Missouri

*258   PROFILE STUDY OF THE AIRFLOW   1965
Collage, pencil, and watercolor, 22×29¾ in.
Provenance : 5
Harry N. Abrams Family Collection, New York

*259   SKETCH OF THE AIRFLOW, FROM A SNAPSHOT (FRONT END)   1965
Crayon, 30×22 in.
Provenance : 5
Collection of John and Kimiko Powers, Aspen, Colorado

260   SKETCH OF THE AIRFLOW, FROM A SNAPSHOT (REAR END)   1965
Crayon, 30×22 in.
Provenance : 5
Louise Ferrari, Houston, Texas

261   THE AIRFLOW—TOP AND BOTTOM, FRONT, BACK AND SIDES, TO BE FOLDED
INTO A BOX (*study for cover of* Art News)   1965
Collage with pen and spray enamel, 17½×17¾ in.
Provenance : 5
Collection of John and Kimiko Powers, Aspen, Colorado

262   SKETCH OF A BOX TO PRESENT SIX VIEWS OF THE AIRFLOW (*study for cover of*
Art News)   1965
Ink, pencil, and watercolor, 9×11¾ in.

*263   THE AIRFLOW—TOP AND BOTTOM, FRONT, BACK, SIDES, WITH SILHOUETTE
OF THE INVENTOR (*original for cover of* Art News)   1965
Collage with pen and spray enamel, 17½×17¾ in.
Provenance : 5
The 180 Beacon Collection of Contemporary Art, Boston, Massachusetts

264   STUDY FOR A SOFT SCULPTURE IN THE FORM OF THE AIRFLOW INSTRUMENT
PANEL, WHEEL, GEARSHIFT, ETC.   1965   [*signed 1967*]
Crayon and watercolor, 30×22 in.
Provenance : 5
Seymour Rapp, Toronto, Canada

265 ⋅ STUDY FOR A SOFT SCULPTURE IN THE FORM OF THE AIRFLOW INSTRUMENT
PANEL, WHEEL, GEARSHIFT, ETC.   1965   [*signed 1967*]
Crayon and watercolor, 30×22 in.

266   STUDY OF RADIATOR FAN AND FAN BELT—THE AIRFLOW   1966
Cut-out drawing, pencil, and spray enamel, 40×25½ in.
Provenance : 5
Mr. and Mrs. Roger Davidson, Toronto, Canada

*267   PATTERNS USED IN THE SEWING OF THE SOFT RADIATOR, FAN AND FANBELT—
THE AIRFLOW   1966
Cut-outs, felt pen, and spray enamel, 40×26 in.
The artist, New York

*268 PATTERN USED IN THE SEWING OF THE SOFT TRANSMISSION BOX—
THE AIRFLOW 1966
Cut-out drawing, pencil, and spray enamel, 25½ × 40 in.

269 STUDY OF A 3-WAY PLUG 1966
Cut-out paper, pencil, and spray enamel, 40 × 25½ in.
Provenance: 3
Dr. Hubert Peeters Van Hoorenbeeck, Bruges, Belgium

*270 STUDY OF A 3-WAY PLUG CUBE TAP—SKETCH FOR A POSTER *(not executed)* 1966
Pencil, 40 × 26 in.
Provenance: 5
Art Institute of Chicago, Chicago, Illinois, Restricted Gift of The Blum-Kovler Foundation

271 STUDY OF A TOILET SEAT AND BOWL—FROM ABOVE 1966
Pencil and watercolor, 36 × 25 in.

272 PROFILE STUDY OF A TOILET BASE—COMPARED TO A MAP OF DETROIT AND
MT. SAINTE-VICTOIRE BY CÉZANNE 1966
Collage and pencil, 34 × 38 in.
Provenance: 5
Cy Twombly, New York

273 THE BATHROOM GROUP IN A GARDEN SETTING 1966
Crayon, pencil, and watercolor, 26 × 40 in.
Provenance: 3
Moderna Museet, Stockholm, Sweden

274 STRANGE, GEOMETRIC MICKEY MOUSE *(used as mask in the performance* Moviehouse
and later as a letterhead) 1966
Spray enamel over stencil, 14 × 14 in.
Robert Fraser, London, England

275 FALLING TEA BAG 1966
Crayon and watercolor, 9 × 11¾ in.
Scott Hyde, New York

*276 FALLING TEA BAG 1966
Crayon and watercolor, 6⅛ × 4¼ in.
The artist, New York

277 SWEDISH DRAINPIPE 1966
Altered newspaper clipping, 17 × 14 in.
Provenance: 5
Arman Fernandez, New York

278 SOFT DRAINPIPE *(drawn for catalogue of* Dine - Oldenburg - Segal *group show at the
Art Gallery of Ontario)* 1967
Crayon, 18 × 14¾ in.
Provenance: 5
Collection of John and Kimiko Powers, Aspen, Colorado

279 SWEDISH WINGNUT 1966
Altered newspaper clipping, 17×14 in.
Louise Ferrari, Houston, Texas

*280 STUDY OF A SWEDISH BREAD—KNÄCKEBRÖD *(for a multiple in cast iron)* 1966
Pencil and watercolor, 24×21 in.
Provenance: 5
Collection of Max Kozloff, New York

281 SAW HANDLE 1966
Crayon and watercolor on cardboard, irregular outline, 44½ in. long
Mr. and Mrs. John Melin, Malmö, Sweden

282 STUDY OF A SWEDISH LIGHT SWITCH 1966
Chalk and watercolor, on cardboard, 64×62 in.

283 PROPOSED MONUMENT FOR KARLAPLAN, STOCKHOLM—TURNING WINGNUT 1966
Photoprint from pencil (original in parts), 11½×15½ in.
The artist, New York

284 PROPOSED COLOSSAL MONUMENT BEHIND THE MODERNA MUSEET, STOCKHOLM—
SWEDISH DOORHANDLE AND LOCKS, TWO VIEWS 1966
Pencil, 11⅝×16½ in.; 11¼×16½ in.
The artist, New York

285 TERMINUS OF PROPOSED NEW BRIDGE, LIDINGÖ, STOCKHOLM, IN THE FORM
OF SWEDISH BATHTUB FIXTURES 1966
Crayon
Provenance: 5
Öster Fagerlin, Mo och Domsjö, Sweden

286 PROPOSED COLOSSAL MONUMENT FOR LÅNGHOLMEN, STOCKHOLM—SAW 1966
Pencil
Archive of Decorative Art, Konsthall, Lund, Sweden

287 PROPOSED COLOSSAL MONUMENT FOR LÅNGHOLMEN, STOCKHOLM—STÄMPEL
(office stamp) 1966
Crayon
Archive of Decorative Art, Konsthall, Lund, Sweden

288 PROPOSED COLOSSAL MONUMENT FOR THE ENTRANCE TO STOCKHOLM HARBOR—
PIVOTING LION 1966
Crayon and watercolor
K.G. Hultén, Stockholm, Sweden

289 FLAG IN THE FORM OF A KNÄCKEBRÖD 1966
Crayon and watercolor, 26×36 in.
Provenance: 5
Daniel Hjorth, Stockholm, Sweden

290 FLAG IN THE FORM OF A SAW 1966
Crayon and watercolor, 26×36 in.
Provenance : 5
Daniel Hjorth, Stockholm, Sweden

291 ELEPHANT HEAD COMBINED WITH OUTBOARD MOTOR 1966
Crayon and watercolor, 18¼×15 in.
Mr. and Mrs. Eric Virgin, Stockholm, Sweden

292 PROPOSED COLOSSAL MONUMENT FOR PICCADILLY CIRCUS—PIPE, LIGHTER, AND
VALISE 1966
Crayon and watercolor, 7½×9¼ in.
Provenance : 3
Gudrun Osmond-Clark, London, England

293 VARIOUS POSITIONS OF A GIANT LIPSTICK TO REPLACE THE EROS FOUNTAIN,
PICCADILLY CIRCUS 1966
Crayon and watercolor, 18×24 in.
Provenance : 5
Collection of John and Kimiko Powers, Aspen, Colorado

294 PROPOSED COLOSSAL MONUMENT FOR THAMES ESTUARY—EAR 1966
Crayon and watercolor, 7×9¾ in.
Provenance : 5
Stolen

295 PROPOSED COLOSSAL MONUMENT FOR THAMES ESTUARY—KNEE 1966
Crayon and watercolor, 15½×22⅛ in.
Provenance : 5
D. and J. de Menil Collection, Houston, Texas

296 PROPOSED COLOSSAL MONUMENT FOR THAMES ESTUARY—KNEE 1966
Crayon and watercolor, 15×22 in.
Provenance : 5
Mr. and Mrs. Dirk Lohan, Chicago, Illinois

297 PROPOSED COLOSSAL MONUMENT FOR THAMES ESTUARY—KNEE 1966
Crayon and watercolor, 15×22 in.
Provenance : 5
Collection of Simone Withers Swan, New York

298 PROPOSED COLOSSAL MONUMENT TO REPLACE THE NELSON COLUMN IN
TRAFALGAR SQUARE—GEARSTICK IN MOTION 1966
Crayon and watercolor, 19×26 in.
Provenance : 5
Private collection, New York

299 PROPOSED COLOSSAL MONUMENT TO REPLACE THE NELSON COLUMN IN
TRAFALGAR SQUARE—GEARSTICK IN MOTION 1966
Crayon and watercolor with magazine clipping, 15×22 in.
Provenance : 5
Mr. and Mrs. Alfred Ordover, New York

300 PROPOSED COLOSSAL MONUMENT FOR THAMES RIVER—THAMES BALL,
VIEW FROM BELOW 1966
Crayon and watercolor, 15 × 22 in.
Provenance : 5
Neil Levine, New Haven, Connecticut

301 THAMES BALL COCK—STAGES 1966
Crayon and watercolor, 15 × 22 in.
Provenance : 5
McCrory Corporation, New York

302 PROPOSED COLOSSAL MONUMENT FOR BATTERSEA PARK—DRUM SET 1966
Crayon and watercolor, 15 × 22 in.
Provenance : 3
Mr. and Mrs. Edwin Bergman, Chicago, Illinois

303 FIXTURE FOR A LONDON TAXI—INTERIOR LAMP IN THE FORM OF AN EAR 1966
Crayon and watercolor, 21½ × 14½ in.
Louise Ferrari, Houston, Texas

304 FAG END 1966
Crayon and watercolor, 7 × 9¾ in.
Provenance : 5
Roy Lichtenstein, New York

305 FAG END 1966
Crayon and watercolor, 7 × 9¾ in.
Provenance : 5
Nathan Gelfman, New York

*306 FAG END 1966
Crayon and watercolor, 15 × 22 in.
The artist, New York

307 FAG END 1966
Crayon and watercolor, 15 × 22 in.
Provenance : 3
Dr. Hubert Peeters Van Hoorenbeeck, Bruges, Belgium

*308 LIGHT SWITCHES, LONDON 1966
Crayon and watercolor, 9½ × 7 in.
The artist, New York

309 CAPRIC 1966
Crayon and watercolor, 14 × 11 in.
Provenance : 5
Galerie Rolf Ricke, Cologne, West Germany

310 PROPOSED MONUMENT FOR OSLO—FROZEN EJACULATION (SKI JUMP) 1966
Crayon and watercolor, 22 × 30 in.
Provenance : 5
Mr. and Mrs. Dirk Lohan, Chicago, Illinois

311 PROPOSED COLOSSAL MONUMENTS—LUNCH BOX CONTENTS ON THE ISLANDS
OF THE UPPER BAY 1967
Crayon and watercolor, 26×40 in.

312 PROPOSED COLOSSAL MONUMENT FOR TORONTO—DRAINPIPE 1967
Pencil and watercolor, 40×26 in.
Provenance : 5
Joseph Kramer, Toronto, Canada

313 PROPOSED COLOSSAL MONUMENT FOR TORONTO—DRAINPIPE 1967
Pencil and watercolor, 22×30 in.
Provenance : 5
D. and J. de Menil Collection, Houston, Texas

314 PROPOSED COLOSSAL MONUMENT FOR TORONTO—DRAINPIPE, VIEW FROM
LAKE 1967
Crayon, 18×24 in.
Provenance : 5
Collection of John and Kimiko Powers, Aspen, Colorado

*315 BASE OF COLOSSAL DRAINPIPE MONUMENT (TORONTO) WITH WATERFALL 1967
Pencil and watercolor, 24¾×22 in.
Provenance : 5
Collection of John and Kimiko Powers, Aspen, Colorado

316 BASE OF COLOSSAL DRAINPIPE MONUMENT (TORONTO) FRONT VIEW 1967
Ink and watercolor, 11×8½ in.
Provenance : 5
Collection of Mr. and Mrs. Michael Blankfort, Los Angeles, California

*317 PROPOSED COLOSSAL UNDERGROUND MONUMENT—DRAINPIPE 1967
Cut-out, pencil, spray enamel, and watercolor, 40×26 in.
Provenance : 5
Mr. and Mrs. M. Riklis, New York

318 PROPOSED COLOSSAL UNDERGROUND MONUMENT—DRAINPIPE 1967
Chalk, crayon, cut-out, and watercolor, 30×22 in.
Provenance : 5
Collection of John and Kimiko Powers, Aspen, Colorado

319 STUDY FOR A SOFT SCULPTURE IN THE FORM OF A DRAINPIPE 1967
Crayon and watercolor, 30×22 in.
Provenance : 5
Dr. William C. Levin, Galveston, Texas

320 STUDY OF A FAN CAGE 1967
Crayon, pencil, and spray enamel, 30×22 in.
Provenance : 5
Mrs. Robert M. Benjamin, New York

321   STUDY OF A SWEDISH LIGHT SWITCH   1967
Crayon, spray paint, and watercolor, 30×22 in.
Provenance : 5
Private collection, New York

322   "CAPRIC"—ADAPTED TO A MONUMENT FOR A PARK   1967
Crayon and watercolor, 22×30 in.
Provenance : 5
Collection of John and Kimiko Powers, Aspen, Colorado

*323   SMALL MONUMENT FOR A LONDON STREET—FALLEN HAT (FOR
ADLAI STEVENSON)   1967
Crayon, 15½×22 in.
Collection of John and Kimiko Powers, Aspen, Colorado

324   SMALL MONUMENT FOR A LONDON STREET—FALLEN HAT (FOR
ADLAI STEVENSON)   1967
Pencil and watercolor, 23×32 in.
Provenance : 5
Collection of John and Kimiko Powers, Aspen, Colorado

325   PROPOSED COLOSSAL MONUMENT FOR THAMES RIVER—THAMES BALL COCK   1967
Crayon, pen, and watercolor on postcard, 3½×5½ in.
Provenance : 5
Ed Janss, Thousand Oaks, California

*326   PROPOSED COLOSSAL MONUMENT FOR THAMES RIVER—THAMES BALL COCK   1967
Crayon, pen, and watercolor on postcard, 3½×5½ in.
Provenance : 5
Carroll Janis, New York

327   PROPOSED COLOSSAL MONUMENT FOR THAMES RIVER—THAMES BALL COCK VIEW
FROM RIVER   1967
Pencil and watercolor, 26¼×40 in.
Provenance : 5
Mr. and Mrs. R.H. Waddell, New York

328   BEACH HOUSE FOR EAST HAMPTON, L.I. IN THE FORM OF A DOORHANDLE   1967
Pencil, 22×30 in.
Carter Burden, New York

*329   PROPOSED COLOSSAL MONUMENT—FAN IN PLACE OF THE STATUE OF LIBERTY,
BEDLOES ISLAND   1967
Pencil, 26×40 in.
Provenance : 5
Steve Schapiro, New York

330   PROPOSED COLOSSAL MONUMENT FOR CENTRAL PARK, N.Y.C.—MOVING POOL
BALLS   1967
Pencil and watercolor, 22×30 in.
Provenance : 5
D. and J. de Menil Collection, Houston, Texas

331 PROPOSED COLOSSAL MONUMENT FOR PARK AVENUE—MOVING BALLS 1967
Pencil and watercolor, 27⅞×22½ in.
Provenance: 5
D. and J. de Menil Collection, Houston, Texas

332 COLOSSAL FAG END IN PARK SETTING 1967
Pencil and watercolor, 30×22⅛ in.
Mrs. Christophe Thurman, New York

*333 COLOSSAL FAG ENDS IN PARK SETTING, WITH MAN 1967
Pencil and watercolor, 30×22 in.
Provenance: 5
Mrs. René d'Harnoncourt, New York

*334 FAG ENDS IN BAG ASH TRAY 1967
Crayon and watercolor, 30×22 in.
Provenance: 5
Mr. and Mrs. Seymour Propp, New York

335 STUDY FOR A SOFT SCULPTURE IN THE FORM OF A GIANT KETCHUP BOTTLE 1967
Pencil and watercolor, 30×22 in.
Provenance: 5
Höglund Collection, Stockholm, Sweden

336 STUDY FOR A SOFT SCULPTURE IN THE FORM OF A GIANT LIPSTICK 1967
Crayon and watercolor, 30×22 in.
Provenance: 5
Mrs. S. Allen Guiberson, Newport, Rhode Island

337 BUILDING IN THE FORM OF AN ENGLISH EXTENSION PLUG 1967
Pencil, 22×30 in.
Provenance: 5
Mr. and Mrs. Arthur Cohen, New York

338 COLOSSAL FAG ENDS INSTALLED ON DOBERMANN ESTATE, WESTPHALIA, WITH
SHEEP-FAG END WATCHING 1967
Pencil, 26×40 in.
Provenance: 5
Mr. and Mrs. Richard L. Selle, Chicago, Illinois

339 COLOSSAL FAG END—DREAM STATE 1967
Pencil, 30×22 in.
Provenance: 5
Mr. and Mrs. Alfred Ordover, New York

340 DRAINPIPE—DREAM STATE 1967
Pencil and watercolor, 30×22 in.
Provenance: 5
Mrs. S. Allen Guiberson, Dallas, Texas

341 LOOKING UP TWO GIRLS AT EXPO '67, LOOKING AT A GIANT BASEBALL BAT, IN FULLER SPHERE 1967
Pencil, 30×22 in.
Collection of John and Kimiko Powers, Aspen, Colorado

342 SELF-PROJECTION INTO WOMAN FIGURE TO CONVEY SENSATION OF GEARSHIFT-OBJECT, WITH MEDUSA ORNAMENTS 1967
Pencil, 26×40 in.
Provenance : 5
Art Institute of Chicago, Chicago, Illinois

343 LYING WOMAN, WITH LEGS APART, REFLECTIONS AND ECHOES 1967
Pencil, 30×22 in.
Provenance : 5
Mr. and Mrs. C.B. Wright, Seattle, Washington

344 STUDY OF HANGING FORM—WOMAN DEMONSTRATING 1967
Pencil, 40×26 in.
Provenance : 5
Mr. and Mrs. Elliott Abrams, New York

345 WOMAN ENTWINED IN GIANT ELECTRIC CORD 1967
Pencil and watercolor, 40×26 in.
Provenance : 5
Lo Giudice Gallery, Chicago, Illinois

346 NUDE WITH ELECTRIC PLUG 1967
Pencil, 26×40 in.
Mr. and Mrs. Richard E. Oldenburg, New York

347 TEA POT—ORIGINAL ILLUSTRATION FOR *Image of the Buddha Preaching* BY FRANK O'HARA *(for the memorial volume published by the Museum of Modern Art)* 1967
Pencil, 2 sheets, each 14×11 in.
Museum of Modern Art, New York

*348 DROPPED CUP OF COFFEE—STUDY FOR *Image of the Buddha Preaching* BY FRANK O'HARA 1967
Pencil and watercolor, 30×22 in.
Museum of Modern Art, New York, Gift of the artist

*349 STRIPPER WITH BATTLESHIP—STUDY FOR *Image of the Buddha Preaching* BY FRANK O'HARA 1967
Pencil, 30×22 in.
Museum of Modern Art, New York, Gift of Mr. and Mrs. Richard E. Oldenburg

350 STUDY FOR THE GIANT SOFT DRUM SET 1967
Pencil, 30×22 in.
Dr. Peter Ludwig, Aachen, West Germany

*351   STUDY FOR THE GIANT SOFT DRUM SET   1967
Pencil and spray enamel, 30×22 in.
Provenance : 5
Collection of John and Kimiko Powers, Aspen, Colorado

*352   DRUM PEDAL STUDY—FROM A SLINGERLAND DRUM CATALOGUE   1967
Pencil, 30×22 in.
Provenance : 5
Collection of John and Kimiko Powers, Aspen, Colorado

*353   DRUM PEDAL STUDY—SCHEMATIC RENDERING   1967
Pencil and watercolor, 30×22 in.
Provenance : 5
Collection of John and Kimiko Powers, Aspen, Colorado

*354   DRUM PEDAL STUDY—VISUALIZATION OF COLLAPSED VERSION   1967
Pencil, 30×22 in.
Provenance : 5
Collection of John and Kimiko Powers, Aspen, Colorado

355   DRUM PEDAL STUDY—PLAN OF PARTS   1967
Pencil and watercolor, 22×30 in.
The artist, New York

356   PROPOSED CHAPEL IN THE FORM OF A SWEDISH EXTENSION PLUG   1967
Crayon and watercolor, 30×22 in.
Provenance : 5
Krannert Art Museum, Champaign, Illinois

357   PROPOSED MONUMENT TO COMMEMORATE CLARENCE DARROW—TYPEWRITER, EMERGING FROM THE LAGOON IN JACKSON PARK, CHICAGO   1967
Crayon and watercolor, 16¾×16⅝ in.

358   PROPOSAL FOR A FLOATING SCULPTURE—GIANT BANANA PEEL   1967
Crayon and watercolor, 30×22 in.

359   PROPOSED COLOSSAL MONUMENT FOR GRANT PARK, CHICAGO—WINDSHIELD WIPER, OVERHEAD VIEW   1967
Crayon and watercolor, 17×12½ in.
Provenance : 5
Louise Ferrari, Houston, Texas

360   PROPOSED COLOSSAL MONUMENT FOR GRANT PARK, CHICAGO—WINDSHIELD WIPER, VIEW FROM LAKE   1967
Crayon and watercolor, 14×17 in.
Provenance : 5
Mr. and Mrs. Richard L. Selle, Chicago, Illinois

361 LATE SUBMISSION TO THE CHICAGO TRIBUNE ARCHITECTURAL COMPETITION
OF 1922—PERPENDICULAR ORE BOAT 1967
Crayon and watercolor, 9¾×7 in.
Provenance : 5
Private collection, Houston, Texas

362 PROPOSED COLOSSAL MONUMENT FOR GRANT PARK, CHICAGO—WINDSHIELD
WIPER 1967
3 postcards (altered by drawing), 3½×5½ in. (each)
The artist, New York

*363 PROPOSED COLOSSAL MONUMENT FOR THE WEST SIDE OF CHICAGO IN THE FORM
OF SMOKE 1967
Crayon and watercolor, 7×9¾ in.
The artist, New York

364 PROPOSED MONUMENT FOR THE SOUTH-EAST CORNER OF NORTH AVENUE AND
CLARK STREET, CHICAGO—BAT SPINNING AT THE SPEED OF LIGHT 1967
Crayon and watercolor, 12×17¾ in.
Provenance : 5
Francis and Sydney Lewis, Richmond, Virginia

*365 LATE SUBMISSION TO THE CHICAGO TRIBUNE ARCHITECTURAL COMPETITION
OF 1922—CLOTHESPIN, VERSION ONE 1967
Crayon, pencil, and watercolor, 22×23¼ in.
Provenance : 5
Philip Johnson, New Canaan, Connecticut

366 LATE SUBMISSION TO THE CHICAGO TRIBUNE ARCHITECTURAL COMPETITION
OF 1922—CLOTHESPIN, VERSION TWO 1967
Crayon, pencil, and watercolor, 22×23¼ in.
Provenance : 5
Charles Cowles, New York

367 FAG END *(to advertise print show to benefit the Foundation for Contemporary Performance
Arts)* 1967
Crayon, 10½×10⅜ in.
Provenance : 5
Dayton's Gallery 12, Minneapolis, Minnesota

*368 SCISSORS IN ACTION 1967
Collage and crayon, 30×20 in.
The artist, New York

369 PROPOSED COLOSSAL MONUMENT TO REPLACE THE WASHINGTON OBELISK,
WASHINGTON, D.C.—SCISSORS IN MOTION 1967
Crayon and watercolor, 30×19¾ in.
Provenance : 5
Philip Johnson, New Canaan, Connecticut

Catalogue Raisonné of Prints, 1960-1967

Asterisks indicate that the print is reproduced in chronological sequence.
Dimensions are sheet size.

I   RAY GUN PUBLICATIONS 1960

1. *Ray Gun Poems*
2. *More Ray Gun Poems*
3. *Spicy Ray Gun*
Various dimensions
Drawings printed by mimeograph and bound at the Judson Gallery, New York
Unsigned and unnumbered

*2   LEGS 1961

Etching, 11⅛×15 in.

Edition: 12
Printed at Pratt Center for Contemporary Printmaking, New York
Publisher: The artist
Signed C.O. 1961 in pencil at the bottom center and numbered from 1 to 12 at the bottom center

*3   ORPHEUM SIGN 1961

Etching, 10×7⅝ in.
Edition: 100
Printed at Georges Leblanc, Paris, in brown-black and scratched on surface
Note: Six artist proofs printed at Pratt Center, 1961, in blue-black on paper 11⅛×15 in., signed A.P. and numbered from 1 to 6
Publisher: Galeria Schwarz, Milan, Italy
Signed Claes O. in pencil at the bottom center and numbered from 1 to 100

4   THREE LITHOGRAPHS 1961

1. *Pie, 22×30 in.*
2. *Store Poster, 19½×26 in.*
3. *Table Top with Objects, 22×30 in.*
Edition: 6
Printed at Pratt Center for Contemporary Printmaking, New York
Publisher: The artist
Some signed C. Oldenburg, others unsigned
Some numbered; some dated October 17, 1961 or October, 1961

5   THREE ILLUSTRATIONS FOR *One Cent Life* (POEMS BY WALASSE TING) 1963

1. *Untitled (for poem "All Kinds of Love," p. 136), 5×7¼ in.*
2. *Untitled (for poem "All Kinds of Love," p. 137), 5×7¼ in.*
3. *Parade of Women, 10¼×14¾ in.*
Lithographs in crayon
Edition: 100 special, 2000 regular
Printed by Maurice Beaudet, Paris
Publisher: E.W. Kornfeld, Bern (1964)
Signed

*6 FLYING PIZZA 1964

Color lithograph, 22 × 30 in.
Edition : 200
Printed by Irwin Hollander, New York
Publisher : Tanglewood Press, New York
Signed Claes Oldenburg in full in pencil at the bottom right and numbered from 1 to 200

7 POSTER ADVERTISING *The Paris Review* — CORNER OF A MATTRESS 1966

Color silkscreen, 25 × 38¼ in.
Edition : 150
Printed by Steve Poleskie, New York
Publisher : The Paris Review, *New York*
Signed Claes Oldenburg in full at the bottom right and numbered from 1 to 150

8 DOUBLE PUNCHING BAG *(to benefit the Foundation for Contemporary Performance Arts)* 1967

Color lithograph, 20 × 38¼ in.
Edition : 80
Printed by Atelier Mourlot, New York
Publisher : The List Art Poster Program, New York
Signed C.O. 67 in pencil at the bottom right and numbered from 1 to 80 at the bottom left (poster version in offset)

9 SCISSORS—AS MONUMENT AND TO CUT OUT *(for the opening of the National Collection of Fine Arts)* 1967

Two color lithographs, each 30 × 20 in.
Edition : 100
Printed by Atelier Mourlot, New York
Publisher : The List Art Poster Program, New York
Signed C.O. in pencil at the bottom right and numbered from 1 to 100 at the bottom left